# pioneers, pedlars, and prayer shawls

RABBI NATHAN MAYER PASTINSKY, Spiritual Leader of the Vancouver Jewish Community, 1918-48.

The citizens of the city of Vancouver mourn the death of Rabbi Pastinsky. For thirty years he devoted his life to this community. How can we best eulogize the man who delivered his eulogies at the biers of our loved ones, now dead and gone?

The reporters speak of his spiritual leadership but we remember rather his worldliness. His religion dwelt not in an ivory tower but in his daily deeds. The obscure, the abstruse, the mysterious symbols, these were not his tools of ministration. His was a single tool, that of understanding the frailties as well as the attributes of mankind. . . .

Stories out of his experience are legion. No branch of society was unknown to him. The officials of immigration, the judiciary, the leaders of state, all respected him. We like to think of the occasion when a famous jurist, sitting as a naturalization commissioner, and seeing a great number of Jewish applicants and Rabbi Pastinsky in attendance asked only: "Rabbi, how many of these applicants belong to your flock." Answered the Rabbi, "Whether they belong to my synagogue or not they are all in my flock." That was the measure of the man. . . .

What more need we say of a man who cared not whether his supplicant was orthodox or reform, religious or non-religious, Jew or gentile; his rule read only, "Was he in need?"*

* From an eulogy by N. T. Nemetz, Vancouver *Jewish Western Bulletin*, 20 February 1948, p. 4.

# Pioneers, Pedlars, and Prayer Shawls

## THE JEWISH COMMUNITIES IN BRITISH COLUMBIA AND THE YUKON

*Cyril Edel Leonoff*

THE JEWISH HISTORICAL SOCIETY OF BRITISH COLUMBIA

SONO NIS PRESS
VICTORIA, BRITISH COLUMBIA

1978

Canadian Cataloguing in Publication Data

Leonoff, Cyril Edel.
Pioneers, pedlars, and prayer shawls

Includes index.
ISBN 0-919462-74-X

1. Jews in British Columbia — History.
2. Jews in the Yukon Territory — History.
I. Title.
FC3850.J5L45 971.1'004'924 C78-002190-8
F1089.7.J5L45

Published by
SONO NIS PRESS
1745 Blanshard Street
Victoria, British Columbia

Designed and printed in Canada by
MORRISS PRINTING COMPANY LTD.
Victoria, British Columbia

# contents

# PREFACE

This collection of photographs from the archives of the Jewish Historical Society of British Columbia, with accompanying commentary, spans the history of the Jewish communities in British Columbia from the earliest days to the present time. The scope of this publication is intended to give a broad-brush picture of the growth and varied activities of the Jewish people in the Pacific Coast province and contiguous Northern region of Canada. The society hopes that this will stimulate a definitive study of the many facets of the communities, which will lead to the writing of a full-scale history at a future time. The background to the present work is discussed below.

David Rome, a B.C. historian, later of the Jewish Public Library and Canadian Jewish Archives, Samuel Bronfman House in Montreal, has made a lifelong study, publishing a book[1] and several articles on the early Victoria-based community, dating from the gold rush of 1858.[2] Minutes of Congregation Emanu-El of Victoria were kept from 1862 to 1931, and are preserved in the Provincial Archives of British Columbia.[3] Being well integrated into American and British ways and prominent in business, community, and political endeavors, the activities of members of the Victoria Jewish community have appeared in the contemporary press and publications.

Vancouver was not established until 1886 but, as the terminus of the transcontinental railway, soon became the main business and population centre of the province. It was natural that, within a short time, Vancouver would house the major Jewish community in British Columbia. The Jews of Vancouver were mostly East European in origin. Victims of *pogroms* and deprivation in their homelands, the newly-arrived immigrants, at the poverty level and unfamiliar with the local language, did not have the facility to keep synagogue or organization minutes. Thus, prior to the establishment of a regular Jewish weekly press in 1930,[4] there have been few written records available of the Vancouver Jewish community.

Arriving at historic truth is a complex matter even if contemporary records were abundant. In 1958, the Centennial year of British Columbia and of Jewish settlement in this province, a start was made by a small committee to collect and record our history. Its work was published in several articles, and highlighted in a B.C. Centenary Edition of *The Jewish Western Bulletin*[5] under the editorship of Abraham J. Arnold.

In 1971, the Centennial year of the entry of the province into Canadian confederation, The Jewish Historical Society of British Columbia was established.[6] The society has continued gathering of archival materials, largely through the taping of oral histories, and collecting personal photographs and documents of the extant pioneers or descendants of pioneer families. Of particular significance, for the first time a record has been collected of the small, but colorful, Jewish communities in the towns and hinterlands of the province.[7]

This publication has been a joint endeavor of the active members of The Jewish Historical Society of British Columbia assisted by several outside people. In particular, the following have made significant contributions to the fulfillment of this work:

A. Myer Freedman, president, whose roots run deeply into the early decades of the Vancouver community, having arrived as a young child in 1914, and been an active participant in community affairs since; he knows personally virtually every extant pioneer of the Vancouver Jewish community; and has collected a great deal of pictorial and archival matter across the continent, from Vancouver to Montreal to California.

Julius Shore, vice-president, who grew up in the Vancouver community, and has done research and writing based on his personal reminiscences from the 1920s through the 1930s; his work of exhibiting displays at archives, libraries, and schools throughout the Lower Mainland and Victoria, and his radio and TV appearances, have done much in publicizing Jewish history and the work of the society.

Allan Klenman, vice-president, Victoria has done a large amount of research and collection on the Victoria community from gold-rush days to modern times.

Irene Dodek, display chairman and Ann Krieger, oral history chairman, as a team were responsible for arranging and presenting pictorial displays, and did taped interviews over a period of five years of the majority of the surviving pioneers; much of their ground work has formed the basis for this publication.

The late Sam Promislow, treasurer for the society's first five years until his death, who always succeeded in balancing the books, often through trying times.

Morris Saltzman, executive-director of Canadian Jewish Congress, Pacific Region, parent body of the society; having a vast store of knowledge of the Vancouver community, he has assisted with factual information and proofreading of the manuscript.

Sam Kaplan, editor and publisher of *The Jewish Western Bulletin*, has made his newspaper and photograph archives available to the author for perusal at all times, and freely publicized the work of the society in the pages of the newspaper.

Willard Ireland, former B.C. archivist, Lynn Ogden, former Vancouver city archivist, and Ron D'Altroy, curator Historic Photograph Section Vancouver Public Library, who made their invaluable collections available to the society.

The scores of pioneers, families, and organizations of the Jewish communities of British Columbia, who created this history and have made their personal reminiscences, photographs, and documents available for use by the society.

Grants to assist the research and publication of this book have been provided by Canadian Jewish Congress, The Carling Community Arts Foundation, and Province of British Columbia Ministry of the Provincial Secretary and Travel Industry — Grace M. McCarthy, Minister.

The author was the founding president and is the current archivist of The Jewish Historical Society of British Columbia. The selection, presentation, and interpretation of the materials is his responsibility.

CYRIL EDEL LEONOFF
Vancouver, British Columbia
*Rosh Hashanah* — Jewish New Year
*Tishrei 5738* — September 1977

*MENORAH* TILE MOSAIC, New Jewish Community Centre, Vancouver, B.C.

# 1

## IN THE BEGINNING

Long ago, Jews from the Orient may have been the first white people to set foot in British Columbia, remaining long enough to leave the imprint of their culture among the Native Indian tribes. Various explanations have been suggested: one story is that the Indians are descendants of a lost tribe of Israel; another is that Jewish war vessels drifted across the Pacific Ocean and landed on the North Pacific Coast of America. Towards the end of the thirteenth century, when the colorful Kublai Khan made his ill-fated expedition against Japan, the story has it that his fleet was dispersed by a storm and blown into the Pacific Ocean. And junks bearing the Jewish contingent of his troops supposedly made the great drift across the Pacific, landing possibly in the vicinity of the Queen Charlotte Islands or the Nass River.[1]

More plausibly, Jewish traders from China may have been amongst the first white people to cross the Pacific and land on the Northwest Coast of America. It is well documented that many ships operating in North Pacific waters bore Jewish names.

In support of these theories, many Coast Indian customs are suggestive of Hebraic ceremonies such as: purification rites, fasting from sunset to sunset, measurement of time and seasons, and customs enforced upon female adolescents. The ceremonial dress of the Medicine Man or Chief is reminiscent of that of the biblical Jewish priest: mitred head-dress, breast plate, and wearing of fringes. Father Jean Marie Le Jeune, Catholic missionary to the Indians and expert linguist, reported that he had discovered Hebrew words in every native dialect west of the Canadian Rockies.[2]

However fascinating, such stories are conjecture rather than history.

The first known Jew said to have settled on British territory in the Pacific Northwest was Adolph Friedman. A native of Latvia, in 1840 at the age of nineteen, the young man embarked for the new world from the port of Libau, with thirty-five Scandinavian sailors. Sailing via the Cape Horn route, after several stopovers, in 1845 they reached the deepwater port of present-day Tacoma, then part of the territory under jurisdiction of the Hudson's Bay Company. Here Friedman became the first merchant, supplying goods to pioneer fishermen. He took up a homestead in the American Lake district, calling his land the "Friedman Addition." The

United States government later built the Fort Lewis army camp on this site. Adolph Friedman travelled to Victoria, British Columbia to marry a relative, Masha Stusser. He passed away at Tacoma in 1911 at the ripe old age of ninety. Branches of the Friedman and Stusser families still reside in Tacoma and Seattle, Washington and Vancouver, B.C.[3]

ANTIQUE SEVEN-BRANCHED *MENORAH*, Temple Emanu-El, Victoria, B.C.

# 2

## VICTORIA: BIRTHPLACE OF THE COMMUNITIES 1858

Within recorded history, the Fraser River gold rush in 1858 brought the first substantial settlement on the British Pacific Coast. Among the settlers were about one hundred Jews. Some came from England and from Australia, seeking adventure and opportunity in developing territories of the British Empire. Most came from California where a sizable Jewish community had become established during the earlier gold rush there. They had come to America in the first half of the nineteenth century, mostly from the German and Austrian dominions, as reformers escaping from reaction. The exodus peaked after 1848 when revolution, unrest, and subsequent reaction, on the one hand, pushed them out of Europe and news of the discovery of gold in California, on the other hand, attracted them to America.

These people were among a class of restless young men and women of great social and ethnic diversity, seeking their fortunes in the western and northern frontiers of North America: from the California gold rush of 1849, to the British Columbia gold rushes of 1858 and 1862, to the last major rushes of the Yukon and Alaska at the turn of this century.

Alfred Waddington, in the first book printed in the Crown Colony of Vancouver Island, a rare first-hand contemporary account of the rush of 1858, expressed his biased Anglo-Saxon contempt for the newcomers:

> . . . Victoria was assailed by an indescribable array of Polish Jews, Italian fishermen, French cooks, jobbers, speculators of every kind, land agents, auctioneers, hangers on at auctions, bummers, bankrupts, and brokers of every description. . . . They came to sell and to speculate, to sell goods, to sell lands, to sell cities, to buy them and sell them again to greenhorns, to make money and begone.[1]

Despite Waddington's harangue, the contribution of the hundred was far greater than could be expected from their small numbers.[2] They were a remarkable group of men and women, perhaps never equalled by any other immigration to Canada. Being educated in England and the United States, having established their position in Anglo Saxon society long before coming to Victoria, they moved about with an easy grace that few minority groups of that era ever attained. Among these pioneers were advisors to governors, legislators, mayors of the major cities, founders of business and industry, philanthropists, and patrons of the arts.[3]

Several Jews started out as miners in the gold fields. However, with their experience and flair in these occupations, the Jews made their greatest contribution as traders, merchants, and wholesalers,[4] supplying first the gold-rush towns, then the cities and industries that sprang up in the province. In search of a livelihood they did not hesitate to work long hours, travel great distances, endure severe hardships, and face dangers.

The port city of Victoria in the Colony of Vancouver Island quickly developed as the principal urban and supply centre for the rush. Here and in the rough-hewn towns that sprang up overnight in the mainland Colony of British Columbia, where the gold was mined, the few Jews represented a substantial proportion of the education, talent, initiative, and business enterprise in the colonies. The Jews, with their adaptability and tenacity, successfully met the challenge of this last frontier of the Pacific Northwest. They established not only the first Jewish community on the British Pacific Coast, but helped to lay the foundations for the union of the two colonies under one government in 1866, and for a new Canadian province in 1871.

The Jews were looked upon by their fellow colonists mainly as better-class Englishmen or Germans, who were different only in religion.[5] Although well integrated into the larger general community in their new frontier locale, these people still maintained a common heritage of Jewish faith, law, social and cultural identity, that served to bind them together as an identifiable group. Within the first year of coming to Victoria, they organized for the purpose of religious services[6] and acquiring a burial ground.[7]

ORNAMENTAL IRON RAILING, Temple Emanu-El, Victoria, B.C.

1. S.S. *PACIFIC*,[8] Brought Gold-Seekers to British Columbia, 17 July 1858: One of the Ships that Transported Thousands of People from California.

When the *Pacific* arrived at Esquimalt harbor on this date she carried twelve hundred passengers, mostly in steerage at thirty dollars a head. Among the seventy cabin passengers was Frank Sylvester, the first recorded Jewish arrival.[9]

2. VICTORIA, VANCOUVER ISLAND, July 1858, As It Appeared to the Hundred Jews Who Arrived During the Fraser River Gold Rush.[10]

3. FRANCIS JOSEPH SYLVESTER, First Jewish Arrival in Victoria, 17 July 1858.[11]

Frank Sylvester[12] from New York crossed the continent overland by stagecoach in 1857 when he was twenty. Arriving in Victoria from San Francisco after a six-day voyage on the *Pacific*, he put all of his money into a small store. When this failed he set out on the long mountainous trek to the gold fields. His diary records thrilling descriptions of this hazardous journey:

> At one time I had to cross a narrow saddle on a trail not less than a thousand feet above the river, a trail not over a foot wide, and the least misstep would have sent me into the boiling river, faintly seen below.

Having no luck in the gold fields either, he returned to Victoria around 1862, finding that more Jews had established in the city. Sylvester became an accountant in the firm of J. P. Davies, an auctioneer, but later established the Sylvester Feed Co.[13]

4. J. P. DAVIES & CO., Auctioneers, Wharf Street, Victoria, V.I. Drawing ca. 1878.

Judah Philip Davies,[14] born and educated in England, spent some years in Australia before coming to California during the gold rush of 1849. In

1863 he moved north to Victoria. Davies was in business as an auctioneer for many years. Prominent in community affairs, he was active in the building of the synagogue, and headed a committee to organize a choir for the dedication services.[15] Davies had four sons and two eligible daughters. The elder, Elizabeth, became Mrs. Herman Schultz in October 1863, in the first marriage held in the new synagogue. A grandson named Samuel, born in 1865, became the first Jew to sit upon the judge's bench in Canada.

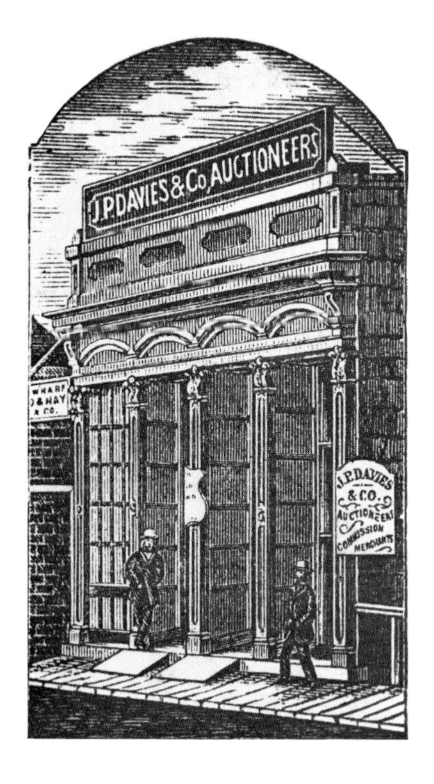

5. CECELIA DAVIES SYLVESTER, Kept "a Jewish Home" in Victoria.

The younger Davies daughter, Cecelia, was born at Sydney, Australia in 1848. In Victoria, she was enrolled in Mme V. A. Pettibeau's "seminary for young ladies." Sylvester, a dozen years older, fell in love with his employer's attractive young daughter. The courtship lasted several years. The couple married in January 1869, occupying their home "Firleigh" on Fisgard Street where they entertained society, including the lieutenant-governor of British Columbia and the canon of the Anglican church. "She was a gentle woman and her home was her castle." An excellent hostess, she played the piano, sang with her husband, and danced well.[16]

In an age where a woman's place was in the home, Cecelia also took a lead in public affairs. Every charitable work in the town held her interest: she was an early member of the Imperial Order Daughters of the Empire, indefatigably collected money for building of the synagogue,[17] worked for the little pioneer French hospital, then served on the executive board of the Royal Jubilee Hospital when it opened.[18]

Frank Sylvester died a respected pioneer in 1908. Cecelia lived on until November 1935.[19] They are buried side by side in Victoria's Jewish cemetery.

6. JEWISH CEMETERY, Cedar Hill Road, Victoria, V.I., Oldest in Western Canada. Consecrated 5 February 1860.

On 18 May 1859 the following meeting notice was published in the press:

> THE ISRAELITES of this city are respectfully invited to attend the meeting at Mr. Simpson's Store, on Yates street, above Broad st., at 3 o'clock P.M., on Sunday, 22d inst., for the purpose of procuring a suitable place for a Burying Ground.
>
> A. BLACKMAN,<br>I. A. BRUNN, } Committee.[20]

Abraham Blackman was an ironmonger and hardware dealer. He was instrumental in organizing the Jewish community of Victoria, giving it much initiative and time.[21] On 5 June 1859 he became founding president of the Victoria Hebrew Benevolent Society,[22] the first Jewish organization in Western Canada. Later he was to become the first treasurer of the congregation, and chanted the *Kol Nidrei* in the first services held in the new synagogue.[23] A founder of the Masonic Lodge of the colony, Blackman arranged for the first participation of the Masons in a public ceremony, the laying of the cornerstone of the synagogue.[24]

Abron Simpson became a charter member of the congregation, and opened its first meeting in 1862. He was elected vice-president in 1863, and blew the *shofar* at the first High Holy Day services that year.[25] Later the Simpson brothers were important merchants of Fairbanks, Alaska.[26]

A. Joseph Brunn was a "fashionable" tailor and clothier, who became a charter member and first trustee of the synagogue.[27]

It is said that Lewis Lewis donated the site of the Jewish cemetery to the community. Born in Poland, Lewis came with his wife to Yale in June 1858 from California. In 1859 he operated a grocery, and from 1861-90 a dry goods store, in Victoria. One of the most important men in Jewish community affairs, he was also a founder of the Masonic Lodge of Victoria.[28] In July 1904 he was buried with Masonic ritual in the historic cemetery that he had helped to found.

On 20 March 1861, a committee of Victoria Masonic Lodge was named to receive the body of Morris Price, a Freemason who had been murdered by Indians at Cayoosh, a gathering place for gold-seekers on the eastern flat of the Fraser River opposite the present town of Lillooet. "The body was received in due course and interred in the Jewish Cemetery with the ceremonies of the Craft."[29] The burial on 6 May 1861 was the "first interment in this cemetery."[30] The first Jewish woman buried was Elizabeth Davies Schultz who died suddenly in November 1866[31] at age twenty-two.

7. TEMPLE EMANU-EL, 1461 Blanshard Street, Victoria, V.I. Canada's Oldest Serving Synagogue, Consecrated 1863.[32] Photo ca. 1890.

The first organized act of the community took place in the fall of 1858 when the Jews of Victoria observed the Jewish New Year and Day of Atonement in a private house on Johnson Street.[33] The first official meeting of the Victoria congregation was held on 15 August 1862 by a committee on subscriptions of the "First Hebrew Benevolent Society," who had purchased a piece of land "suitable in all respects for $730," for a future synagogue.[34]

Five years after their arrival, the young Jewish community erected a house of worship. The congeniality with which the Jewish people were accepted in early Victoria may be judged by the following facts. Many non-Jews contributed to the building fund of the synagogue.[35] The laying-of-the-cornerstone ceremony on 2 June 1863 was attended by all creeds and nationalities of the community. Mayor Thomas Harris and Chief Justice David Cameron walked in the procession. The cornerstone was laid "plumb," "level," and "square" by Right Worshipful Master Robert Burnaby of the Masons. The Germania Sing Verein, the Hebrew Benevolent Society, the French Benevolent Society, the St. Andrew's Society, the Fraternity of Ancient and Honorable Order of Freemasons of Victoria and Vancouver Lodges, and the band of H.M.S. *Topaze* from Esquimalt, all participated in the ceremony.

The Victoria newspaper devoted a large part of its next issue to report the ceremony, concluding:

> Thus terminated an eventful day in the history of the Jews in Vancouver Island and it must be a source of infinite gratification to that body, that the ceremonies of this day, partaking as they did of an exclusively denominational character were participated in by all classes of our community, with a hearty good will and brotherly feeling, evidencing in acts

more powerful than words, the high estimation in which they are held by their fellow-townsmen of the city of Victoria.[36]

On 13 September 1863 the Temple building was completed and the actual consecration took place. On this occasion the sermon was delivered in English by Rev. Dr. Morris R. Cohen, first rabbi of "The Emanuel of Victoria, Vancouver Island."

8. ABRAHAM HOFFMAN, First Synagogue Secretary.

The Hoffman family were active in the congregation. Abraham was the first secretary when the congregation was formed, and held this position for many years. Vice-President Samuel Hoffman made the address on the occasion of the cornerstone laying:

> Who would have thought that, in the short space of five years, we should have a temple erected where then the aborigines were the lords of the domain? Who would have dreamt that in this isolated part of the globe, where, ere now, the foot of white men had hardly trod, there should spring up a comparatively large city, studded with magnificent edifices, and inhabited by a large concourse of intelligent people? Who would not have ridiculed the idea that where, ere now, nought but the hunter's step and wild beasts' roar ever disturbed the wilderness, should, at this early day, be erected a synagogue by the scattered tribes of Israel? . . . It is easy to remember the advent of the first Israelite. Nevertheless, scattered as our race are all over the world, and limited in numbers, as we generally are, compared to our Gentile brethren, I am proud to say, that since we first

made our appearance, one by one, we have each and all striven manfully to uphold that religion which has been handed down to us by our forefathers.[37]

9. INTERIOR TEMPLE EMANU-EL, Victoria, B.C. Photo ca. 1902.

The interior of the temple is shown in its original form. It had a lofty ceiling with a glass dome in the middle and balconies for the women. A large adjoining hall was built where they held synagogue socials, with classrooms for teaching the children.[38] Today, 114 years later, the temple still serves as the centre of Jewish religious and community life in Victoria. It is the oldest standing synagogue building in Western North America.

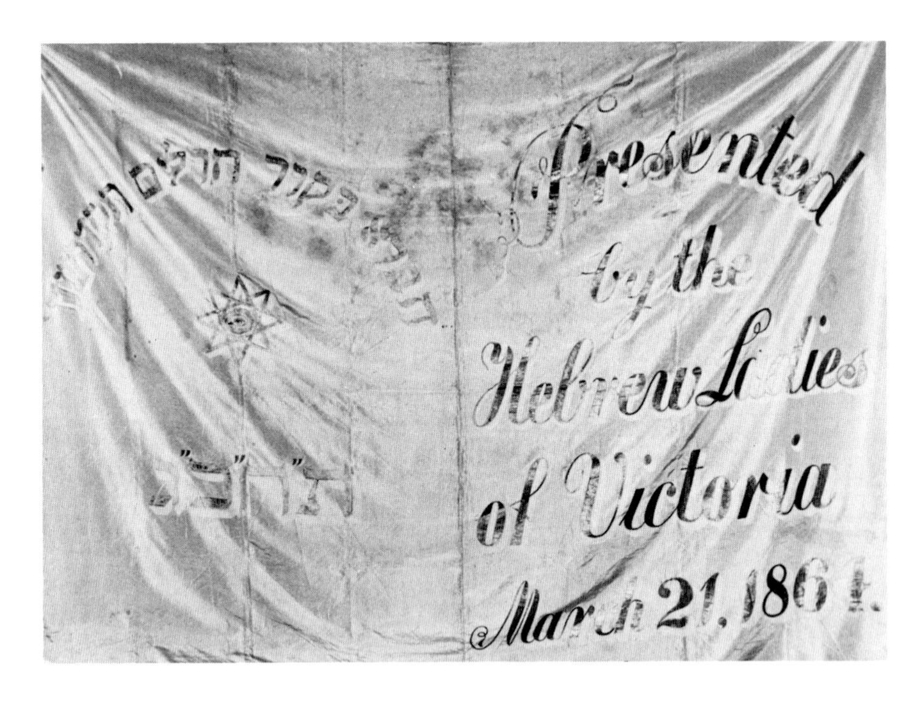


10. WEDDING CANOPY, Presented by the Hebrew Ladies of Victoria, 21 March 1864.

Made of silk from China, manufactured in England, and transported by ship around Cape Horn to Victoria, it was used for congregation marriages until recent times.

The Chief Rabbi's Pastoral Tour.
1920
1921
UNION OF SOUTH AFRICA.
COMMONWEALTH OF AUSTRALIA.
DOMINION OF NEW ZEALAND.
DOMINION OF CANADA.


11. VERY REV. DR. J. H. HERTZ, Chief Rabbi of the British Empire, Visited Victoria and Vancouver, July 1921.

Autographed copy of tour brochure presented by the rabbi to his hosts, Mr. and Mrs. Joseph Rose of Victoria.

From the outset, the Victoria congregation maintained a British tie. Shortly after formation, Sir Moses Montefiore and Baron Lionel de Rothschild, two leaders of Anglo-Jewry who resided in London, were appointed as honorary members. In February 1863 communication from London was received by David Shirpser, first president of the congregation, written by Chief Rabbi Dr. N. M. Adler, along with a pastoral letter "circulated among all the Hebrew congregations in the British colonies."[39]

The first pastoral tour of commonwealth countries by a British chief rabbi was made in the interest of the Jewish War Memorial Fund for religious education, in memory of Jewish soldiers who fell in World War I. Fifty thousand Jews had fought under the flag of the Empire, and five Victoria Crosses were won. The tour "excited wide interest." The chief rabbi was officially welcomed by Lieutenant-Governor W. C. Nicol and Premier John Oliver. He addressed the Canadian Clubs in Victoria and Vancouver, being warmly received in both communities.[40]

12. RABBI MARCUS BERNER, Pioneer Rabbi of the West, Served at Hirsch and Victoria in the Period 1899-1941.

Marcus Berner was a pioneer rabbi of Western Canada. Minister of a congregation in England, he had joined the tide of Jewish emigration to North America. In 1899 settling at Hirsch, one of the earliest Jewish farm settlements in Saskatchewan, he farmed his homestead, serving also as teacher and religious leader of the colony. In 1931 Rabbi Berner came to Victoria to serve as spiritual leader of the congregation for the last ten years of his life.[41]

13. TIGER ENGINE CO., No. 2, Officers, Victoria, V.I. Photo 1864.

"There was no remuneration when these men answered the alarm. They toiled for the honor of the force, striving with rival companies to lay first water on the blaze."[42]

Belonging to the fire brigade was fashionable in those days. Frank Sylvester (seated centre) was secretary. Another Jewish member was Henry Emanuel Levy (standing left), who was also a police officer under Commissioner A. F. Pemberton.[43]

The press reported in 1929 that "Henry Levy . . . is the only surviving member of Victoria's first volunteer fire brigade, and one of its most respected citizens."[44] He died that year at the age of eighty-six.

## 14. VICTORIA LODGE No. 758, INDEPENDENT ORDER OF B'NAI B'RITH, Executive, with Julius Benjamin Jaffe, President, 1917.

*Top L to R:* S. Flash, warden; J. Rose, treasurer; I. Waxstock, p.p. and district deputy; H. Comm, assistant monitor; S. Glazan, guardian.
*Bottom L to R:* H. H. Brown, trustee; J. Katz, vice-president, J. B. Jaffe, president; J. Dobrin, secretary; E. P. Nathan, trustee.

Aside from religious institutions, B'nai B'rith, a Jewish men's service organization, is the earliest international Jewish organization in British Columbia. The third B'nai B'rith lodge in Canada was Victoria Lodge No. 365 organized in 1886,[45] which was succeeded by this lodge, instituted on 19 July 1914.[46]

## 15. FIRST COMMUNITY PASSOVER SEDER, Victoria, B.C., 1917, Took Place Under Auspices of the B'nai B'rith Lodge.

Dr. Sigfried Moritz Hartman (1858-1923), old-time Jewish dentist in Victoria, is chairing the head table. He was always active in the synagogue,

had a good voice, and officiated capably when no rabbi was available. He had joined the Klondike gold rush to Dawson City in 1897.[47]

16. A PRINCE AND HIS DRIVER, Victoria, B.C., 1919.

Benjamin Grossman (at the wheel) was given the honor of chauffeuring Edward, Prince of Wales (rear seat left) during the royal visit to Victoria.[48]

In 1907 Grossman brought the first Oldsmobile touring car to Victoria, using it as a "rent car" (taxi). In the automobile business most of his life, with seventy years of driving, Ben is regarded as B.C.'s oldest motor-car man. At age ninety-two he is also Victoria's oldest living Jewish citizen.[49]

17. GAMBITZ'S, First Dry Goods and Drapery Store, 43 Yates Street, Victoria, V.I. Drawing 1862.

Kady Gambitz opened his first store in 1858 on the west side of Yates Street. In December 1859 he opened a new store on Yates near the corner of Government Street. The store is shown in this engraving (second from left), between the Adelphi Saloon and the Bank of British North America. Gambitz remained in the business until he left the colony in 1865, selling the store to Thomas and William Wilson, who for many years conducted the business as the "City House."[50]

18. LOWER YATES STREET, Victoria, V.I. Photo 1860s.[51]

Many pioneer businesses were located on this street. Among them were: the premises of Joseph Boscowitz, pioneer Jewish fur dealer; and the famous first tobacco business in British Columbia founded by Gustave Sutro, "the leading wholesale tobacco merchant of Victoria."[52]

In 1858 the Boscowitz fur store on Wharf and Bastion Streets was one of the first business establishments in the city. The firm became leader in the sealing industry, operating three ships in the North Pacific. By the time of his death at Victoria in 1923 in his eighty-ninth year, Joseph Boscowitz, over a period of sixty-five years, had played a remarkable part in the economic development of the province.[53]

The Sutros, of Prussian-Jewish descent, were a legendary Pacific Coast family. Adolph was head of the family in the United States. Gustave and Emil were among the first Jews in Victoria, taking a prominent part in all aspects of the community life.[54]

19. SIMON LEISER-WHOLESALE GROCER, 14-16 Yates Street, Victoria, B.C. Photo 1880s.

Leiser came to Victoria circa 1877 and set up as a grocer. By the 1890s he conducted the largest wholesale business in British Columbia, employing over one hundred people on Vancouver Island. For fifteen years Simon Leiser served on the Victoria Board of Trade, being president for two terms. He was an executive member of the Vancouver Island Publicity Bureau.[55]

Leiser, a German Jew, was to encounter the age-old Jewish problem of nationality. In World War I, when the *Lusitania* was torpedoed by a

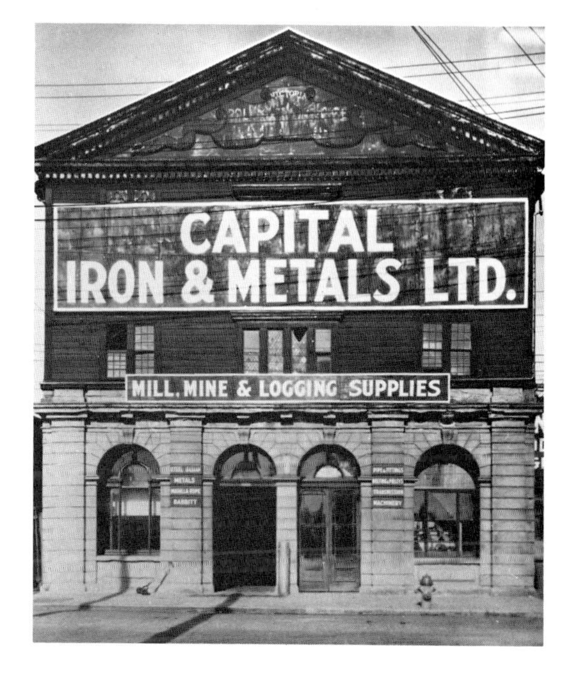


German U-boat, taking down with her fourteen passengers from Victoria, a mob raided the premises of several persons of German ancestry, among them Leiser's grocery.[56] For this purpose the assailants regarded him as a German rather than a Jew or a Canadian, though he had resided in this country for over thirty-five years.

20. J. ROSE JEWELER-GRADUATE OPTICIAN, Victoria, B.C. Photo ca. 1912.

Joseph Rose graduated in optics from Bradley Polytechnic Institute, Illinois in 1912 and practiced in Victoria. Marrying Sonia Robinson of Vancouver in 1918, the Roses have been a prominent Jewish family in Victoria for over sixty years.[57] Rose's Jewelers, still operated by the family, is a leading business on Douglas Street today.

21. CAPITAL IRON & METALS LTD., Mill, Mine & Logging Supplies, 1824-32 Store Street, Victoria, B.C. Photo 1930s.

This business, started by Harry Wagner and Isidor Stein in the early 1930s, is continued today by the Morris Greene[58] family. It stocks a prolific variety of marine hardware and ship chandlery.

22, FREDERICK LANDSBERG, Chosen "Best Citizen" of Victoria, May 1930.

Fred Landsberg, one of a family of seventeen, was born in Russia in 1859 of Orthodox Jewish parents. He served as a youth in the Russo-Turkish war. Coming to Canada under the Baron de Hirsch[59] scheme, he landed at Victoria in 1884 with a capital of five hundred dollars. Succeeding in the real estate business, he became a leading philanthropist.[60] He was awarded the Appreciation Medal, given by the Victoria Post of the Native Sons and Daughters of British Columbia, to the "best citizen" of Greater Victoria,[61] and the Jubilee Medal in 1933.[62]

23. HARRY LOUIS SALMON, Centenarian, 1858-1958.

Born in London, England, Salmon came to Victoria in 1884. Starting out as a reporter on the *Colonist*, with English financing he built the Salmon Block at Government and Yates Streets, where he operated a tobacco store. Originally Solomon, the name changed to Salmon as a result of trading with the Indians. He gained fame for originating the "Salmon Sweepstakes" based on the English Derby and other horse races. Tickets sold for one dollar, with results posted on the windows of his store. During seventy-four years in Victoria, Salmon participated in numerous general and Jewish community activities, serving every position in Temple Emanu-El from *shammes* to president.[63] He passed away in his hundredth year during B.C.'s Centennial year.[64]

24. ALICE MALLEK, Honored with Centennial Medal, Victoria, B.C., July 1958.[65]

Mrs. Mallek is being congratulated by Mayor Percy Scurrah on receiving the British Columbia Centennial Medal for "having enriched the lives of her fellow citizens." Residing in Victoria since 1913, she was an active business woman,[66] at one time being the only woman member of the Victoria Chamber of Commerce. Following her husband Harry and son Eddie, she became president of Congregation Emanu-El, being the first woman to serve in such capacity in Canada.[67] Mrs. Mallek also carried out a successful campaign to restore Victoria's historic Jewish cemetery when it fell into a state of disrepair.

25. B.C.'S OLDEST LIVING NATIVE-BORN JEWISH CITIZENS, Empress Conservatory, Victoria, B.C. Photo 23 July 1972.

Cousins Daisy (Salmon) Minchin (left) and Josephine Lancaster (right) were born at Victoria in 1892 and 1893 respectively, delivered by "Dr. Jim" Helmcken. Mrs. Minchin, at the time of the photograph, was visiting from California for the Seventieth Anniversary reunion of Victoria College — then affiliated with McGill — of which she was a member of the 1910 class.[68] Mrs. Lancaster has spent her entire eighty-four years living in Victoria.

# 3

# NANAIMO

26. ALEXANDER MAYER, Proprietor of "the Red House — the Pioneer Store," Nanaimo, V.I., from 1863-90.

Bypassing the highly competitive Victoria, Alexander Mayer of Portland arrived at Nanaimo in 1861 with two large trunks of goods to establish a clothing store. The monopoly of the Hudson's Bay Company, which owned all of the land comprising Nanaimo at that time, prevented him from doing so. Not to be thwarted, he opened the trunks on the nearest street corner and sold out in a short time. Returning with another selection of dry goods, he opened a shop in the lobby of the Miners' Hotel and sold out once again.

In 1863, finding lots on the market selling by public auction, he purchased one with a log building on it for six hundred dollars. Thinking the structure drab, he mixed up a can of paint, adding what he thought was a touch of red. Forevermore, it was known as "Mayer's Red House — the Pioneer Store." The general store became a success from the start. He was joined in business by two sons-in-law, Sam Levi and Marcus Wolfe. Mayer retired in 1890 and died in Nanaimo four years later at the age of eighty-one, leaving an estate valued at $14,500.[1]

27. MARCUS WOLFE, Grand Master of the B.C. Grand Lodge of the Masons, 1891-92.

Marcus Wolfe was born in California. In 1861, at age sixteen, he arrived at Yale where he worked for the Oppenheimers. Settling in Nanaimo a short time later, Wolfe became secretary of the Water Works and Board of Trade. He married Bertha Mayer, and became a partner in his father-in-law's firm, Alexander Mayer & Co. After sale of the firm in 1893, he entered the real estate and insurance business.[2]

On their arrival at Vancouver Island, Jewish people were active participants in the Masonic Order. Victoria Lodge was organized in August 1860, "the first lodge of the Order ever established . . . in any part of the British possessions on the Pacific." Among "the names of the office bearers" were K. Gambitz and L. Franklin.[3] "During 1860, nine Brethren became members of the Lodge by Affiliation . . . while the first and only person to be made a Mason in the year 1860 was John Malowansky, a Russian news agent and tobacconist."[4] Malowansky, a Jew, was active in community affairs including treasurer of the synagogue in 1863, president of the *Chevra Kadisha*, and a member of the volunteer fire department. Of the twenty-one members of Victoria Lodge in its first year, six were Jews.[5] Lumley Franklin became Worshipful Master of Victoria Lodge in 1865,[6] while Henry Nathan, Jr. held the same office in 1869,[7] and was first Junior Grand Warden of the Grand Lodge of British Columbia on its inception in 1871.[8] Solomon David Levi became the first Worshipful Master of Caledonia Lodge, Nanaimo when it was instituted in November 1867.[9] Edward Collins Neufelder was Grand Secretary of the Grand Lodge of British Columbia from 1884-87.[10] Marcus Wolfe rose to the top of the Masonic Order in British Columbia becoming the thirteenth Grand Master,[11] the only Jewish grand master in B.C. thus far.

28. UNION BREWERY, John Mahrer Master Brewer, Nanaimo, B.C. Built 1891.

John Mahrer was born in 1847 at Prague, Austria of a Jewish distilling family. Coming to America in 1867, he spent two years in the California and Arizona gold fields, and lost money continuously. Returning to San Francisco, he made arrangements to go to Chile, booking passage on the vessel *Shillahoff*. By an accident of fate, he was unable to board ship. The

vessel was wrecked on the journey and all hands, save the captain, were lost.

In the fall of 1870 Mahrer came to Nanaimo. The following year he went to the Cariboo, where he opened a bakery and restaurant. Returning to Nanaimo in 1876 he started a bakery business, a soda-water factory, a soap factory, and in 1879 established a brewery, which became "one of the principal breweries in the province."[12] In 1891 Mahrer's brewery amalgamated with the Union Brewing Co., where he continued as manager and master brewer. He also had interests in the Northern Canning Co. and in a number of gold mines in B.C.

John Mahrer was a leader of the Nanaimo community. He served on City Council for eight consecutive years, was president of the Water Works Co. and a director of the Gas Co. He participated in most of the social and fraternal orders in the city: Masons, Odd Fellows, Foresters, Knights of Pythias, Ancient Order of United Workmen, Legion of Honor, and the City Band. Mahrer died at Nanaimo in September 1912.[13]

29. ALEXANDER SERETH (right), Pioneer Jewish Lumberman, Eureka Sawmills Ltd., Nanaimo, B.C. Photo 1940s.

Born and educated in Austria, where he learned the business as a lumber inspector in 1892, Sereth came to Canada in 1903. He founded a number of logging and sawmilling businesses in Alberta and British Columbia, and was active as a lumber broker. In 1941 he established this mill in Nanaimo. His niece Helen Olfman, who ran the Nanaimo operation, was one of the few women executives in the lumber industry.[14]

Nanaimo continues to have a small number of Jewish residents to this day.

# 4

## NORTHWEST COAST

30. S.S. *BARBARA BOSCOWITZ* (foreground), One of Many Ships in the North Pacific Bearing Jewish Names.

This 396-ton vessel was used by the Boscowitzes' firm for seal hunting in the North Pacific. In a long and useful career, the ship was also engaged in the northern-coast trade from Puget Sound to Skagway.[1]

A traveller on board the ship in 1886 has left a vivid description of the journey:

> We all embarked on the *Boscowitz*, the most miserable, dirty little steamer imaginable. . . . She starts at no regular date, and takes her own time, her average speed being five or six knots an hour. . . . the cabin swarmed with cockroaches, which are repulsive enough when occasionally found in the kitchen, but almost unendurable when as bed-fellows . . . At breakfast the food was so badly cooked and appeared so uninviting, that it was with difficulty we could induce one another to partake of anything . . .
>
> The voyage we found tedious and monotonous . . . owing to the slow pace and delays . . . our vessel was crowded; the saloon with prospectors and adventurers . . . The remainder of the boat was filled with all sorts and conditions of men and women, including several Indians, one of whom was dead . . .[2]

31. BRITANNIA MINE, Upper Workings, Jane Camp. Photo Early 1900s.

In 1898 a trapper discovered "a mountain of copper" along the east shore of Howe Sound, thirty-five miles north of Vancouver. Joseph Boscowitz and sons took a leading part in the early financing and development of this property, selling out to a syndicate in 1903. The camp at level 1050, the famous "Jane claim," was founded by the Boscowitzes.[3] A giant in the development of B.C.'s mining industry, by the time the mine closed in 1974 it had produced more than fifty million tons of 1.25 percent copper ore, which yielded in excess of one billion pounds of copper for the world market.[4]

32. MORRIS MOSS, Adventurer.

Even in the days of great romance the adventures and misadventures of Morris Moss were unequalled. Born in London, England of a well-to-do Jewish family, and educated at University College, he was a handsome man with a well-trimmed beard, correct British accent, cultured tastes, and impeccable manners. Moss, twenty-one years old, arrived at Victoria in April 1862 by way of Panama and San Francisco, as agent for the fur traders Liebes and Co. of that city. From the start he fitted well into the polished society of Victoria with its balls, symphony concerts, and theatrical performances under the aegis of Governor James Douglas.

But Morris Moss, the man of action, was happiest on schooners in northern waters and on the trail, wearing his favorite garb — buckskins. A lanky man over six feet tall, of great courage and determination, essentially a loner and ascetic, he was well equipped for this life. Since boyhood he had avidly read and been fascinated by tales of the Pacific Northwest. His idol was Sir Alexander Mackenzie, who had reached the Pacific overland via the Bella Coola Trail, three-quarters of a century earlier. In England Moss had become a good horseman, an excellent shot, and knew something about sailing. In San Francisco he had learned the rudiments of the fur trade.

Within a few months of arrival in Victoria, against all advice, Moss started a trading post at Bella Coola, but found that smallpox had killed off nine-tenths of the native population. Undeterred, he opened up Mackenzie's old trail and, with the help of Indian guides, ran pack trains through to the miners at Williams Creek and Barkerville. He was greatly respected by the natives, because he observed their customs of sharing food and clothing, and abstained from the white man's practice of taking Indian women to wife.

Back in Victoria late in the year for supplies, Moss was befriended by Governor Douglas, who appointed him Government Agent for the Northwest Coast and Justice of the Peace. On the return trip along the West

Coast his schooner was shipwrecked during a winter gale. Marooned on an island for three months, Moss lived a Robinson-Crusoe existence, was held prisoner by local Indians, then rescued by friendly Bella Coola Indians. Finding his post in shambles and his goods unaccounted for, Moss returned to Victoria broke, surprising his friends who never expected to see him alive again.

In 1864, when Alfred Waddington attempted to build a road from Bute Inlet on the coast through to the interior, the Chilcotin Indians, alarmed at the prospect of losing their lands, and fearful of return of the white man's plague — smallpox, killed most of the road crew in what became known as the Chilcotin War. Moss was summoned by Governor Frederick Seymour to act as "Indian expert" advisor to the British Columbia Legislative Council at New Westminster. As guide, he accompanied the punitive expedition in which several of the murderers were brought to justice. Seymour afterwards appointed him Indian Agent and Deputy Collector of Customs for the Northwest Coast. In this capacity Moss visited nearly every place in British Columbia from the Nass River down.

In 1867 Morris Moss left government employ and became a fur trader at Bella Bella, where he built a store and residence on the site of the old Hudson's Bay Company fort. While prospecting there he discovered the "Hebrew Mine" on which he devoted much time and money; offered twenty-five thousand dollars for a half interest he refused, and in the end never made a cent out of it. The year 1869 found Moss running a trading post in the Queen Charlotte Islands. In 1870, during the "Omineca excitement," he took a canoe to the head of navigation on the Skeena. That fall he fitted out and accompanied a party to search for rich claims near the Alaska boundary.

In the early 1870s Moss bought his first sealing vessel, sailing aboard her every season. This developed into the largest fur and sealing business in British Columbia, and led to his most far-reaching adventure. His two schooners, *Black Diamond* and *Lillie*, were seized in Bering Sea by officers of the United States, which claimed monopoly for the sealing industry. This incident nearly precipitated a war between the States and Canada over sealing rights. The matter was concluded by international arbitration in Paris, in which the U.S. paid full damages to Moss for the illegal seizure.

Morris Moss returned to the social life of Victoria, served as president of the synagogue, the B'nai B'rith Lodge, and the Victoria Club. He built a fine home on Fort Street. Regarded as an eminently eligible but confirmed bachelor, when Moss was forty-two years old he began visiting the home of Mr. and Mrs. Herrman Bornstein — a prominent Victoria dealer in hides and furs, with business interests in San Francisco — paying marked attention to their twenty-two-year-old daughter Hattie. Moss's surprise marriage, at San Francisco in 1883, to the girl young enough to be his daughter became the talk of Victoria. A year later their son Alexander — named after his hero — was born. Moss, apparently feeling confined and restless in domestic life, frequently absented himself on prospecting trips. On a morning in June 1892, Morris Moss left Hattie and their eight-year-old son at home in Victoria to investigate a mining property in Washington State, and the family never heard from him again. News was received of his death in Denver, Colorado four years later.

Alexander Moss, a bachelor, died in Vancouver on 26 February 1968 at age eighty-four, leaving no heirs to perpetuate the name of perhaps the Pacific Northwest's most colorful pioneer. However, the family name lives on in Moss Street, Victoria, Moss Bank and Moss Passage, in Milbank Sound.[5]

33. LANDING A CARGO OF FURS, Louis Ripstein (top right) Trading in Raw Furs, Prince Rupert, B.C. Photo ca. 1910.

Prince Rupert, terminus of the Grand Trunk Pacific Railway and the shortest route to the Orient, was envisioned as Canada's great North Coast deepwater port — rivalling Vancouver. By 1909 a townsite was laid out and incorporated, having a projected population of fifty thousand. The first transcontinental train arrived in April 1914.

From the beginning a small Jewish community formed, comprised of raw fur traders, merchants, and a tailor. Religious services and holiday celebrations were observed in private homes. Beth Jacob was the name given to this smallest of congregations. Planting its stake in the future of

CLOTHING
DIRECTOR, COHEN

NO CREDIT

British Columbia, the Jewish community of Prince Rupert raised a sizable sum of money to help furnish the new General Hospital.[6]

With the onset of World War I and the post-war depression, Prince Rupert was relegated to the status of a branch line. Finding little opportunity, the original Jewish community dispersed by the 1920s, although individual Jewish residents are there to this day.

34. DIRECTOR, COHEN & CO., Pioneer Jewish Clothing Business, Third Avenue, Prince Rupert, B.C. Photo 1910.

*L to R:* Mr. Grossman, Louis Ripstein, Harry Frome, Charlie Cohen, Maurice Cohen, Isidor Director, William Zackon, Morris Soskin.

In 1908, before Prince Rupert was incorporated, its first Jewish residents Isidor Director and Maurice B. Cohen, starting out as squatters, established the first Jewish business in Northern British Columbia.[7]

Born on the border of Germany and Prussia in 1875, Director emigrated to the United States at age seventeen, where he worked in the mines of Michigan. He came to Canada in 1899, living in Winnipeg and Sault Ste. Marie before coming to British Columbia. The Director family spent fourteen years in Northern B.C., becoming leaders in the community. They spent the World War I years in the Prince George district but returned to Prince Rupert from 1918-22, where he became a longshoreman.

Isidor Director had an insatiable curiosity about the land. At one time he walked the 450 miles between Prince Rupert and Prince George "to see the country."[8]

35. LANDO'S GENERAL STORE, Second Avenue, Prince Rupert, B.C. Photo ca. 1913.

Nathan Lewis Lando (left) and brother-in-law David Scheinman (right).

Nathan Lando, an immigrant from England, followed the railway construction, sleeping in tents in sub-zero weather. Arriving in Prince Rupert circa 1911 he opened this store. He began trading with the Indians in raw furs and argillite carvings — then valued at one dollar per inch. Some of these pieces are said to be in the famous Lipsett collection.[9]

Coming to Vancouver in 1921, members of the Lando family have continued in the retail fur and Indian curio business to this day. A son, Esmond, made a significant contribution to opening up the Northwest Coast when "in the wake of the war canoe" he was a founder of Queen Charlotte Airlines in the early 1940s.

Scheinman returned to London in 1914 to enlist in World War I. Later he became known as David David of Malta.[10]

36. PRINCE RUPERT FUR & HIDE CO. LTD., W. Goldbloom "The Trappers Friend," Third Avenue, Prince Rupert, B.C. Photo 1921.

William Goldbloom was a legendary "character" who spent thirty-five years trading furs up and down the Pacific Coast from Victoria to Skagway. With his wide-brimmed Stetson hat and white beard, bearing a striking resemblance to the American folk hero, he was affectionately known as "Buffalo Bill."

A *Litvak*, Goldbloom arrived at Montreal in the 1870s. He "put a pack on his back and followed the CPR out to Winnipeg," where he was one of the earliest Jewish settlers. About 1905 he moved to Vancouver with his wife Rachel and two daughters. He couldn't stay put and he couldn't go any farther west, so he headed north five hundred miles to Prince Rupert at the time of its founding. He became an institution there, running his business through ups and downs until he was eighty-eight years old.

During World War II, Goldbloom's home in Prince Rupert became a haven for Jewish servicemen. One of the most moving experiences of his long and colorful career occurred when he conducted a Passover *seder* for 150 Army and Air Force personnel of both the Canadian and American forces.[11]

# 5

# NEW WESTMINSTER AND THE FRASER VALLEY

"The Royal City" named by Queen Victoria, Capital of the Colony of British Columbia, took form in 1859. From its first days, Jewish citizens have been associated with New Westminster, which was the principal city and river port of the mainland. The names of the New Westminster Jewish firms of Meyer, Reinhardt & Co., and Messrs. (Solomon David) Levi and Boas "suppliers to the Cariboo gold fields,"[1] have come down to us from the early days.

After the establishment of Vancouver in 1886 as the terminus of the transcontinental railway, the importance of New Westminster declined. However in 1904, when the first bridge across the Lower Fraser River was built there for rail and road traffic, New Westminster became the bridgehead, farmers' market, and supply centre to the Fraser Valley. Several Jewish-owned shops established along Columbia Street, the main downtown business thoroughfare, and a significant Jewish mercantile presence exists there to this day.

Following World War II, the small Jewish merchant group was augmented by ex-servicemen, mainly professional people, and a viable Jewish community comprised of twenty families became established, large enough to support a Hadassah chapter and a small Talmud Torah school.[2] With the suburban expansion in recent years, the Jewish community has enlarged and organized under the name Burquest to include Burnaby, New Westminster, Port Moody, Coquitlam, and Surrey.

37. SIMON REINHARDT, Jewish Pioneer of the Lower Mainland at Derby and New Westminster.

Reinhardt in 1858 established a wholesale liquor business in Victoria. But he is best known for his activities in the Lower Mainland. In November 1858 he bought one of the first lots at Old Fort Langley (Derby), which was projected to be the capital of the new Colony of British Columbia, and paid $725, the highest price at the sale. However, when New Westminster was chosen instead, he was associated there with Morris Meyer in a store on Scott's wharf. The firm also bought real estate in New Westminster, at one early sale paying a record $3925 for a lot.[3]

38. MRS. SIMON REINHARDT, Lady of Society.

We first hear of Mrs. Reinhardt in 1855 when she was elected treasurer of the Ladies' Benevolent Society of San Francisco, which had been formed by the "German Jewish ladies to extend aid to German-speaking needy."[4] In Victoria she was a member of the Hebrew Ladies Society and on the general committee of the Female Infirmary. Active with her husband in community affairs, they entertained in their Humboldt Street, Victoria home.[5]

39. ROYAL CITY HADASSAH, Installation of Officers Luncheon, New Westminster, B.C., ca. 1949.

*Back L to R:* Esther Lesk, Leah Lewis, Meta Zalkowitz (top), Frances Panar, Eva Toban, Betty Obtover, unidentified, Eva Lewis, Ruth Zack.
*Middle L to R:* Sonia Panar, Clara Rice, Dina Zack, Gerry Biely, Bessie Waterman, Sarah Teitelbaum, Dina Messe.
*Front L to R:* Mazie Margulius, Bessie Panar, Babs Cohen, Ruth Hardin, Esther Davis.

This women's organization, still operating today, has provided the core of Jewish community life in New Westminster and district. Mrs. Louis (Dina) Zack was founding president from 1947-50.[6] Well known and

beloved by all, the elder Zacks participated in the business and social life of New Westminster, being leaders of the Jewish community there for twenty-five years.[7]

40. PACIFIC PINE CO. LTD., Queensborough, New Westminster, B.C. Photo 20 July 1968.

Jewish people were predominant in the lumber business in Central Europe. When the region was overrun by the Nazis, some brought their skills to Canada. Educated at Cambridge, England with degrees in economics and engineering respectively, Sam and Paul Heller operated the family's business, one of the top lumber producers in their native Poland. They moved to New Westminster in 1941 and developed this sawmill complex.[8]

Samuel Heller served two terms as president of the British Columbia Lumber Manufacturers' Association,[9] travelling abroad in promotion of B.C. lumber products. On retirement he was honored with a citation by the Council of Forest Industries for "outstanding personal contribution to the British Columbia lumber industry from 1941 to 1970."[10]

123
ISLAND TUG

ARMY
AND
NAVY
DEPT. STORE
TABAN'S
QUALITY SHOE STORES
SHOES
REGAL
TABAN'S
SHOES
Rob Roy
MEATS
WOSK'S
ARMY & NAVY
FURS

41. JEWISH MERCANTILE BUSINESSES, Columbia Street, New Westminster, B.C. Contemporary Photo.

ARMY AND NAVY DEPARTMENT STORES

Born in San Francisco in 1897, Sam Cohen, British Columbia's "Merchant Prince," began his empire in 1919, when the young man heard that the stock of a men's clothing store in Kamloops was for sale. He took the train up to the interior city, bought the stock, and rented a location on Hastings Street, Vancouver. Two years later he started the Army & Navy store in Regina as a war surplus outlet and mail order house "to sell goods at a price people can afford to pay." At the time of his death in Vancouver, December 1966, the business had grown into one of Western Canada's largest department-store chains with stores in five cities.[11]

TOBAN'S QUALITY SHOE STORES

Samuel Toban, a small-town shoemaker in Lithuania, came to Vancouver in 1910. He opened a shoe repair shop on Davie Street near Burrard Street. His sons Harry and Dave started working for their father, saved up money, then started out on their own selling shoes on Main Street. From this small beginning, the chain of Toban's Shoe Stores was established throughout Metropolitan Vancouver.[12]

REGAL CLOTHIERS

Choosing a name in keeping with the royal theme of the city, this men's wear store was established by Louis Zack in 1934. Born in Russia, Zack had travelled all over the world before landing in New Westminster in 1912, where he worked for the David Spencer Co. The business, carried on by son Sam "one of the last of his breed — an independent storekeeper," was operated by the Zack family for forty years.[13]

WOSK'S

Born in Odessa, Russia, Ben Wosk came to Canada at age sixteen. In 1932, with borrowed capital, he started a small appliance store with his brother Morris at 1263 Granville Street. Wosk's Ltd. has grown into a public corporation, listed on the Vancouver Stock Exchange, whose holdings include fourteen furniture and appliance stores, and four major hotels in British Columbia.[14] Ben Wosk was named 1973 "Businessman of the Year" by Vancouver Junior Chamber of Commerce, and 1975 "Good Citizen of the Year."[15] Morris Wosk is a leading philanthropist and community benefactor.

**AUCTION SALE**

**2000 ACRES**
**FINE FARMING LANDS**

**J. P. Davies & Co.**

Have received instructions from Alex. Munro, Esq., Chief Factor of the Hudson Bay Co., to sell by Public Auction

**On Monday, 17th June,**

AT 12 O'CLOCK, NOON.

At Salesrooms, Wharf street, that fine tract of land known as the

**HUDSON BAY COY'S FARM,**

Near the Townsite of Langley on South bank of Fraser River,

NEW WESTMINSTER DISTRICT.

Containing 2,000 Acres, in Lots of 100 Acres, more or less, to be sold on a

**Credit of Four Years**

The Property is exceedingly well situated in a thriving settlement traversed by the New Westminster and Yale Waggon Road. The Soil is of very superior quality and most of it is ready for the plough. A large extent has been FENCED, cultivated, and provided with

Commodious Barns, Cattle Sheds and other Buildings.

To Farmers and others this is a most favorable opportunity of securing desirable homesteads.

Lithograph Maps, with all information appertaining to the same, will be furnished on application to

J. P. DAVIES & CO.,
ap9 Auctioneers.

42. J. P. DAVIES & CO. AUCTIONS HUDSON BAY COY'S FARM, Langley, B.C., 1878.

Fort Langley was first built in 1827 on the south bank twenty-five miles upstream from the mouth of the Fraser River. Supply depot of the fur trade, on 19 November 1858 it became the birthplace of British Columbia when the Crown Colony was proclaimed there. In December 1858 Samuel Price, a Jewish businessman of substantial means, contracted to supply the government with lumber for its buildings at Langley.[16]

The area's first large-scale farm of two thousand acres was developed to supply the HBC posts. Fifty years later, when commerce had bypassed it, the farm was subdivided and sold.[17] This replica of the auction notice is displayed in the "Big House" of Fort Langley National Historic Park.

43. GRANDVIEW POULTRY FARM, 3995 Grandview-Douglas Highway, Burnaby, B.C. Photo 1945.

George Biely (in photograph) came to British Columbia in 1932 from Chita, Siberia. After attending UBC Faculty of Agriculture, he developed and operated this six-acre hatchery and egg farm from 1936-60. With seven thousand Leghorn chickens, he supplied the Metropolitan Vancouver area. Hatching eggs were marketed as far away as California.[18]

A brother Professor Jacob Biely, a distinguished researcher, became Head of the Poultry Science Department at the University of British Columbia, and a Fellow of the Royal Society of Canada.[19]

Another major producer was Panco Poultry, developed by Ted Cohen in the Newton district of Surrey, B.C.

44. SAMUEL SUSSEL FARM, Chilliwhack, B.C. Photo ca. 1947.

Jewish people have not taken to farming in British Columbia in significant numbers as they did in the homesteading days of Canada's Prairie Provinces, where substantial Jewish farm settlements were established. However, through the years a dozen Jewish farm families have been identified in the Lower Fraser Valley, mostly new immigrants. There have also been a number of Jewish cattle dealers, meat packers, fruit and vegetable wholesalers.

Sam and Anne Sussel left Hitler's Germany in 1935, when they were prevented from practicing their professions of law and paediatrics respectively. They first visited Palestine with a view to taking up land there, but found the hot climate unsuitable. In 1941 they settled on the land in Chilliwhack Municipality. Sussel (on tractor), forty-seven years old and

knowing little about farming at the outset, developed a mixed-farming operation of Jersey and Guernsey milk cows, Leghorn chickens, and a fruit orchard.[20]

45. TALLACRES FARM, 4670-256 Street (Coghlan Road), Aldergrove, B.C., 1947-68.

This 160-acre dairy farm developed and operated for over twenty years by Nathan J. Tall, with a completely automated milking system, was a model for its time attracting study and tour groups from Canada and the U.S.A. The barn was built in 1947 by a crew of thirty men at a cost of fifty thousand dollars.[21]

46. WERNER BICK WITH HOLSTEIN HERD, 7435-264 Street (County Line Road), Aldergrove, B.C. Photo July 1976.

Bick left his native Germany in 1938 at age nineteen. Arriving in Santiago, Chile with his father, they farmed a rural district and operated a cheese factory for thirty years. Wife Ingrid joined him after spending the war years in Russian camps. In 1969 the Bicks moved to British Columbia's Fraser Valley. Together they operate a 62½-acre dairy farm with 125 head of Holstein cattle.[22]

# 6

## GOLD: FRASER RIVER — BARKERVILLE

47. EARLY VIEW OF YALE, Gateway to the Gold Fields, Fraser River, B.C.

The five Oppenheimer brothers, Meyer, Charles, Godfrey, David, and Isaac, born in Bavaria and educated at the Collegiate school at Frankfurt *am* Main, truly rank as one of British Columbia's extraordinary families. With unrest and revolution sweeping Europe in 1848, when the youngest brothers David and Isaac were in their teens, they emigrated to America. They travelled through frontier country in Ohio, Louisiana, Texas, and California before being caught up by the "gold fever" spreading through British Columbia in 1858.

Fresh from the California gold rush and experienced in the kind of supplies that would be needed by the miners, Charles, apparently the first to arrive and founder of the family firm, established a trading business at

Victoria and Point Roberts. Joined by the other brothers, they set out for the wild B.C. interior, where gold was being mined from the bars of the Fraser. They were shrewd enough to appreciate that sure gold lay not in the mines but in creating a mercantile empire to service them.

At Yale, the head of navigation on the Fraser, by 1859 the Oppenheimers established their main store in a brick building located on the main street facing the river. The store became a gathering place for prospectors and miners during the long, hard winter. The Oppenheimers also began business operations that year at Fort Hope, and in 1860 established a branch at Lytton.[1] Old-time residents there recall other notable Jewish pioneers of Yale: packers, pack-train operators (the Lenhardts and Mr. Saul), merchants, and road builders.[2]

48. BARKERVILLE, Before the Great Fire of September 1868.

The frontier towns are now gone — except as museums — replaced by planned, organized, efficient, often sterile, modern communities. They sprang up from the grass roots to fill the basic needs of the time. Though unplanned, cluttered, inefficient, and usually dirty they had character, attracted men of adventure, and tolerated their eccentricities.

In 1862 a sailor named Billy Barker struck a thousand dollars worth of gold in one foot of ground in British Columbia's Cariboo. A new town Barkerville sprang up, which became the largest community west of Chicago and north of San Francisco. Here the Oppenheimers opened another store, which became the commercial centre of the town.

Several Jewish people were associated with the Cariboo gold-rush towns. Along with the Oppenheimers the most prominent were Carl Strouss, who ran large stores in Barkerville and Williams Creek, and Felix Neufelder of Barkerville, Van Winkle, Richfield, and Soda Creek. Neufelder not only accumulated a sizable fortune, but also devoted his tremendous energies to various public causes such as the fire brigade and the hospital, and served on practically every grand jury between 1867-74. He was active in arranging the popular celebrations for July first and fourth, both observed with equal gusto by the multinational population.[3]

49. ISAAC OPPENHEIMER, Fire Chief, Barkerville, B.C., ca. 1869.

We have some idea of the Oppenheimers' holdings when Barkerville burned to the ground and they lost $100,000 in the blaze. David went to San Francisco to buy a fire engine and Isaac became captain of the fire brigade.[4]

50. CHARLES OPPENHEIMER, Cariboo Wagon Road Builder, 1862.

In every stage of its history, transportation has been the primary requisite in development of mountainous British Columbia. The Oppenheimers became important links in the chain between Victoria and the frontier. They travelled regularly to and fro, carrying gold from the Cariboo to the government in Victoria, crossing Hell's Gate Canyon and over Jackass Mountain, having narrow escapes in evading hostile Indians and outwitting armed highwaymen, leaving a legend of amazing courage and enterprise.

Walter Moberly, pioneer surveyor, explored the possible routes and recommended to Governor James Douglas, and Colonel Richard Moody of the Royal Engineers, a road along the banks of the Fraser and Thompson Rivers. Charles Oppenheimer, of the "great mercantile firm of Oppenheimer Bros.," with his friend Thomas B. Lewis, petitioned the Governor to build the road, seeking to provide the necessary communication among the various units of the family business. In 1862 the firm of Oppenheimer, Moberly, and Lewis obtained a charter to build the 146-mile section from Lytton to Lac La Hache. The Cariboo Wagon Road, the first road into the interior of British Columbia, was successfully completed through to the gold fields.[5]

51. PLACER GOLD MINING, Barkerville, B.C. Photo 1937.

Jack Spaner, son of a pioneer Prince George family, who lived for periods from the 1930s-50s in the Wells-Barkerville district, is seen (centre) with his colleagues at their sluice box, placer mining for gold.[6]

# 7

## SOUTHERN INTERIOR

Unlike Canada's Prairie Provinces, where almost every town had its Jewish storekeeper, the small towns of British Columbia did not attract Jewish settlers in any numbers. This is particularly true of the Okanagan, with its parochial environment, which for many years harbored few diverse-ethnic residents. The main exceptions were the frontier towns of Prince Rupert and Prince George, and Rossland-Trail, which had a stable economy based on the smelter industry.

From the earliest days there was always the odd Jewish person in the Kootenays connected with the mines or the land. People of the district still recall "Silver King Mike" who, before the railway came, earned his living as a packman carrying the personal goods of miners into the mountains. He graduated to a small store in Nelson, stocking mostly working men's clothes. Even the Mayor of Nelson bought gloves from Mike rather than in a more fashionable — perhaps more costly — store. He was a kindly man beloved by children. With great affection his wife called him "a diamond in the rough." They took immense pride in their son, a doctor in New York.[1]

However, it was not until the depression era of the 1930s that a small Jewish community formed in the Rossland-Trail region, composed of merchants, and professional people connected with the smelter. For nearly two decades this became the only viable Jewish community in British Columbia, outside of the Lower Mainland and Victoria, having an organized Jewish community life.

### 52. TRAIL CREEK LANDING, For Riverboats Travelling the Columbia River, and BRITISH COLUMBIA SMELTING AND REFINING CO. (right). Photo 1897.

Few people today are aware that the smelter operations at Trail were started by a man having Jewish origin. Frederick Augustus "Fritz" Heinze was born in Brooklyn, N.Y., his father being apparently of German-Jewish descent.[2] Graduating as an engineer from Columbia School of Mines in 1889, he went to Butte, Montana where he found the richest copper vein, built a smelter, and became known as the "Copper King of Montana." A shrewd, handsome, personable man of powerful build, he was "equally at ease in a group of miners, in cultured society, and in the gambling dens of Butte." Arriving at Trail Creek Landing in the summer of 1895, just twenty-six years old, he built a two-furnace copper smelter blown in on a wintry morning in February 1896, at a forty-acre site on benchland above the Columbia River.[3] It was designed by James Breen. The smelter's superintendent, Herman C. Bellinger, is also reputed to have been of Jewish descent.

Heinze built a narrow-gauge railroad from the boat landing at Trail, eighteen miles inland to the mines at Rossland. Organizing the Columbia & Western Railway Co., with plans for a railroad to the coast, he obtained concessions from the Dominion Government to 300,000 acres of mineral and agricultural lands.

In 1898 the smelter and railroad interests were sold to the Canadian Pacific Railway Co. for a reported $1,200,000,[4] and became the forerunner of the Cominco smelting and fertilizer complex at Trail.

OFFICIALS, British Columbia Smelting and Refining Co., Trail, B.C. *Standing L to R*: James Breen, Charles R. Leonard, W. A. Kidney. *Sitting L to R*: Herman C. Bellinger, Frederick A. Heinze.

53. MAX WOOGMAN, At Woogman's Men's, Ladies' Wear, and Grocery, Rossland, B.C. Photo ca. 1938.

The Woogman brothers, Max and Joseph, from Drumheller, Alberta were two of the earliest Jewish residents of Rossland-Trail in the modern era. Coming in 1932, they operated grocery and clothing stores in Rossland and Trail over a period of thirty years.[5]

54. LEOPOLD LEVEY, President of Trade and Merchants Association, Examines a Silver Brick as He Leads Rossland-Trail Businessmen on Tour of Cominco Smelter, Trail, B.C., ca. 1946.

Leo Levey was a prominent leader within the Trail community. He served in a variety of service groups, was secretary-treasurer of the Trail-

Tadanac Hospital Board and served on the B.C. Hospital Association Board. An organizer of Trail Junior Chamber of Commerce, he became its president and later honorary president. His most notable community achievement was in charge of disaster relief services during the flood of 1948, for which he received the Red Cross Medal of Service. On his retirement in 1968, for thirty-two years of service to the Trail community, Leo Levey was recipient of the "Citizen of the Year" award.[6]

55. ROSSLAND-TRAIL JEWISH COMMUNITY BANQUET, ca. 1948.

Rossland-Trail had a unique Jewish community. Though isolated the twenty-two families, active participants in the community at large, tenaciously practiced their Judaism. A Jewish Benevolent Society was formed to support community endeavors; and a Sunday religious school was taught by parents. Keenly Zionist oriented, the community managed to support a Hadassah chapter,[7] a branch of the Zionist Organization, and a Young Judaea group. Their zeal was internationally recognized when Israeli speakers would stop over to address the small community. *Yom Kippur* was celebrated in a rented hall, with services usually led by Leo Levey who had received training in his native Leeds, England. A rabbi was brought in from Spokane to perform special events such as circumcision and marriage.

56. SAM WISE, "Garlic King of the Kootenays," Rossland, B.C. Photo August 1964.

Samuel Wise lived in Rossland-Trail from 1935-67. On a plot of land behind his hardware store in Rossland, he grew "the most beautiful garden in town." He is seen in his garlic field, which supplied the large Italian community and restaurants in town.[8]

57. FIRST JEWISH WEDDING IN TRAIL, 23 March 1947.

"Everyone pitched in" to help this milestone event of the Jewish community, which united in marriage Clara Wise of Rossland and Charles Waldman, a research chemist at the Trail smelter.[9]

58. WALKERS' JEWELRY STORE, Nelson, B.C. Photo. ca. 1915.

Jack and Martha Walker operated this sophisticated small-city jewelry in the early decades of this century. Martha (second from right) was a Heppner, who in 1886 had been one of the earliest Jewish homesteading families in Western Canada.[10]

# 8

## NORTHERN INTERIOR

59. FIRST AUTOMOBILE TRIP TO B.C. NORTHERN INTERIOR, Was Made by Jewish Residents, 1911.

The start of surveys for the Grand Trunk Pacific Railway from Fort George to Prince Rupert, through the Nechako and Bulkley Valleys, heralded a land boom. George H. Salmon, Managing Director of the Dominion Stock and Bond Corp., conceived the bold adventure of an automobile trip from Vancouver five hundred miles distant to Fraser Lake, along the route into the interior known as the Yukon Trail. Here are seen on a wooden bridge en route Salmon (standing) with his father-in-law Adolph Robinson (the bearded gentleman) who helped to finance the venture.[1]

## 60. ENCOUNTERING DIFFICULTIES ALONG THE YUKON TRAIL, Summer 1911.

The last stagecoach had come through in 1910, and this was the first attempt to drive automobiles over the trail. The trip was made in two cars, a Canadian-made McLoughlin and a small Dodge. George Salmon has described this pathfinding journey:

> On our trip we encountered a great many difficulties along the road. We had to pull out a lot of stumps along the trail to make it possible for the car to pass, and the hills were so great that in many places we had to pull the car up with a block and tackle.
>
> The mosquitoes were so terrible at that time of the year that we had to wear a muslin protection over our heads and faces. We finally arrived at Fraser Lake with the Dodge. The McLoughlin became disabled along the way.

A townsite of nine-hundred acres was subdivided fronting Fraser Lake, and a hotel, general store, and bank were built. The company sold one-million dollars worth of lots in the new town of Fort Fraser, projected as a major trade centre for the railway. The last spike was driven there by the chief engineer before fifteen hundred persons on 5 April 1914, but with the outbreak of World War I the project remained unfulfilled.[2]

## 61. COHEN-ZACKON & CO., Outfitters to Men, New Hazelton, B.C. Photo ca. 1912.

In the years 1912-16 Maurice B. Cohen and William Zackon established a chain of men's clothing stores in towns along the Grand Trunk Pacific Railway at New Hazelton, Smithers, and Telkwa.[3]

62. JACOB LEITH, Patriarch of the Prince George Jewish Community, from 1914-66.

Prince George and District has had a small Jewish population from its first days to the present, but only sporadically large enough to support any organized Jewish community life. The most active periods were during World War II with stationing there of Jewish servicemen, and through the 1950s to mid-1960s when a pulp mill, gas line, and other industrial developments increased the city's population from seven thousand to fifty thousand. By this time there were sufficient Jewish residents to form a *minyan*.

Coming to Canada from Russia with only $3.50 in his pocket, in 1914 Jacob Leith arrived at Prince George where he became a hardware merchant. Residing there for fifty-two years, he was an active servant of the community, working for Chamber of Commerce and service groups. For his contribution to militia, civil defence, and victory loan sales, he was recipient of a certificate of appreciation by the Government of Canada "in the War against the German Reich." Mr. Leith is remembered as the "learned old gentleman" who read the *Torah* at Jewish religious services.[4] He passed away in 1969 at age ninety-four.[5]

63. SPANER'S MEN'S WEAR, Isaac (left) and Louis (right), Third and George Streets, Prince George, B.C. Photo ca. 1935.

The Spaner family came from Rumania at the turn of this century and homesteaded in the vicinity of Winnipeg. The four sons moved west and were involved in fur trapping and trading northwest of Edmonton, Grand Prairie, and Fort George.

Isaac Spaner worked as a chef on the Grand Trunk Pacific Railway construction west of Edmonton, then opened men's wear stores along the route. He did his first business out of a tent at Edson, Alberta then opened stores there, at Wolf Creek, and Fort George. In 1914 he opened the first men's wear store in Prince George.[6] This store, still operated by a branch of the family, has been in continuous operation since inception of the city. Brother Louis continued in the fur business.[7]

64. HOMESTEADING SISTERS, Hannah Director (right) and Rhoda Goldberg (left), Twenty-Two Miles South of Prince George. Photo ca. 1914.

Mr. and Mrs. Isidor Director moved to South Fort George in 1913. At the outset of World War I, Director found it difficult to obtain employment because of his German national origin. So they took up a homestead south of town on the Fraser River. Though accustomed to the conveniences of a large city — she was born and grew up in Montreal — Hannah Director with her three young children endured all sorts of primitive conditions. They lived in a log house with a packed dirt floor. Mrs. Director taught school to the children by correspondence. Supplied by a little riverboat in the summer, when the river froze over in the winter he had to backpack in supplies the twenty-two miles from town.[8]

Returning to Prince George in 1917, the Directors shared in building the town, entering both civic and musical activities. Mrs. Director was the first woman elected a school trustee in Prince George and became Chairman of the Board.[9]

65. SOLDIERS AT FIRST COMMUNITY *SEDER* HELD IN PRINCE GEORGE, B.C., Spring 1943.[10]

Servicemen, their wives, and members of the local Jewish community participated in the traditional festivities of Passover. Canadian Jewish Congress arranged for the necessary supplies of *matzos*, *Haggadahs*, and other essentials at this "far northern outpost" of British Columbia. Corporal William Nathanson was Master of Ceremonies, while Mr. H. Schwartz of Prince George led the *seder* services, following which a sermon was delivered by pioneer resident Mr. Jacob Leith. Both evenings were climaxed with singing of Hebrew songs and the *Hatikvah*.[11]

66 ROSH HASHANAH, Prince George, B.C., 1955.

*L to R:* Lou Simkin, Jack Horlick, Lawrence Shatsky, Harry Greenhut, Sam Arbour, Harry Brown, Moe Arbour, Charlie Graham, Gerry Saunders, Jack Spaner, Morris Spaner.

With outside assistance from Ben Billinkoff of Winnipeg — a lumber buyer at Prince George — who donated the *Torah*, *talisim* sent by a relative in the United States, *sidurim*, and a *shofar* from Rabbi Bernard Goldenberg of Vancouver, the Prince George community held religious services on the Jewish New Year.[12] Charles Graham who acted as *chason* was trained by the rabbi in the ritual for the services.[13]

67. "JOHNNY THE JEW," Gets Surprise Welcome, Vancouver Airport, 1 November 1955.

John Berman (right), age eighty-eight, legendary Jewish trapper of Fort St. James, arrives in Vancouver to take up residence at the Jewish Home for the Aged of B.C. He shows his surprise at being greeted by newsmen and photographers. Sam Shine (left), president of the home, and Mrs. E. Allman (centre), director of the Jewish Family Welfare Bureau, met him at the airport. Popularly known as "Johnny the Jew," originally from New York, he spent forty years in the bush as a recluse until discovered by the Prince George Jewish community.[14]

# 9

# YUKON: FROM KLONDIKE DAYS — ONWARD

Jewish people continued to participate in opening up the last frontiers of the North. Jews in substantial numbers from all over the world were involved as prospectors, miners, and merchants in the last great gold rush to the Klondike River, Yukon Territory in 1897-98. In Dawson City, which sprang up as the commercial centre of this rush, with a population of thirty-five thousand at its peak, over sixty Jewish names have been authenticated.[1]

The first Jewish religious services in the Territory, *Rosh Hashanah*, attended by about forty persons, were held in a store in Dawson on 17, 18 September 1898.[2] The following *Yom Kippur* services were held in the Yukon Pioneer Hall.[3]

68. HENRY MARCOE ZIMMERMAN, Prospector, Yukon Territory, 1898-1940s.

Zimmerman came from San Francisco and staked a claim on Selwyn Creek, Y.T. in 1898. Then he joined the rush to Nome, Alaska. He returned with his nephew, and continued to mine the claim over a period of forty years. Henry Zimmerman was found dead in his burned-out wilderness cabin in the early 1940s.[4]

69. ARTHUR ZIMMERMAN, Gold Miner, Working the Family Claim, Selwyn Creek, Y.T. Photo 1930.

70. LOUIS BRIER, Unknown Community Benefactor, Lynn Valley, North Vancouver, B.C. Photo 1921.

Louis Brier was a native of Rumania, who went to the gold fields of the Yukon shortly after the stampede of 1897. He engaged in general supplies for the miners, and also grubstaked prospectors on a percentage basis.

After making a "rather bulging bankroll," he settled at Lynn Valley in the North Vancouver mountains. The owner of the "first and only steam motor car in Lynn Valley . . . he disposed of it before it blew up." Mr. Brier is seen in front of the commercial and residential building he erected at the northwest corner of Mountain Highway and Lynn Valley Road.

Built of granite block salvaged from an old bank building in Vancouver, the Louis Brier Block became a landmark. Despite a petition by local residents for preservation, it was demolished in 1972 to make way for a service station.[5]

Louis Brier died in 1936 at age seventy-five. Virtually unknown to the Jewish community in his lifetime, he left it a sizable legacy — one-third each for a Jewish old folks' home, orphanage, and a hospital, stipulating that all were to be non-sectarian.[6] It took years before discovery and litigation of the will. On 22 December 1968 the Louis Brier Home for the Aged of B.C. and Extended-care Hospital was dedicated, providing a model for geriatric care in the province.[7]

71. JEWISH CEMETERY, Dawson City, Y.T.

"Bet Chaim," the gate of the Jewish cemetery at Dawson, believed to originate from the Klondike days.

72. HAROLD HILLEL KOFFMAN, Yukon Pioneer. Photo Spring 1934.

Koffman (centre) is seen arriving in the Yukon from Vancouver in the then record time of three days via boat and White Pass Airline. He spent nine years as an electrician, helping to build and maintain the fleet of gold dredges and power lines with Yukon Consolidated Gold Corp., later going into business in Whitehorse.[8] He resided twenty-two years in the Yukon before moving to Vancouver.[9]

# 10

## PIONEERS IN MEDICINE

73. DR. SAMUEL BLUMBERGER, Pioneer Jewish Physician, Practiced in B.C. for Fifty-Three Years.

The first practicing Jewish physician in British Columbia was Dr. M. H. Boscowitz who arrived on the steamer *Pacific* 16 February 1863. He offered his services as a "German Physician, Surgeon and Obstetrician" who is "familiar with the English, French, and Spanish languages."[1]

The first Jewish physicians to practice in Vancouver were Drs. Samuel Petersky and Samuel Blumberger.

The Petersky family can be traced in Vancouver city directories back to 1892 when Simon Petersky was a confectioner, tobacconist, and fruit seller for several years at 37-39 Cordova Street. Sam Petersky was the first Jewish son from Vancouver to study medicine. After graduation from McGill he practiced in Nelson. Dr. Petersky had his first Vancouver office in a building on the southeast corner of Union and Main Streets, below Robert Blumberg's ladies' dress and lingerie factory. Later he relocated to 615 West Hastings Street — near Granville Street — where he practiced as a physician until his sudden death in 1932 while delivering a speech.[2]

Samuel Blumberger, born in Riga, Latvia arrived in America at age fourteen. On graduation from McGill about 1906, he first travelled to the Orient as a ship's doctor, and on one of the cruises met his future wife. Landing at Vancouver in 1909, he practiced medicine for over fifty years in the Dawson (later Ford) Building, 193 East Hastings Street (at Main Street), until his death in 1962 at age ninety.[3]

74. MANITOBA MEDICAL COLLEGE, First Year Class, 1911-12, William Morris (second row, third from right).

The next Jewish doctor to arrive was William Morris. Born in Russia, he came to Winnipeg in 1908, and graduated from Manitoba Medical College as the gold medalist in 1916. On graduation, Dr. Morris came to British Columbia, practicing at Michel and Tranquille before establishing a permanent practice at Vancouver in 1925. Dr. Morris practiced in B.C. a total of forty years until his death, becoming well known as a chest specialist.[4] Stories are told of the occasions when, instead of sending poor patients a bill, he would leave money behind for the purchase not only of medicine but food as well.

A founder of Conservative Judaism in Vancouver, Dr. Morris served as president of Congregation Beth Israel.[5] His wife Rachel (Seidelman) was the first executive-secretary of the Vancouver Jewish Community Chest in 1924-25.[6]

75. THIS DOCTOR TRAVELLED TO HIS PATIENTS BY DOG TEAM, Atlin, B.C. Photo 1925.

Dr. Maurice Fox from Port Arthur, and trained at Manitoba Medical College, came to British Columbia to practice medicine in July 1923. "Following my internship at the Vancouver General Hospital, I fulfilled part of the Lord's promise to Abraham — I inhabited one corner of the earth, namely a remote corner of B.C." Having a wanderlust he worked in several small towns, then married and settled down in Atlin in the years 1925-26.

Working at a three-bed Anglican hospital with two nurses, on a government salary of three hundred dollars a month, Dr. Fox served a population of five hundred miners, trappers, lumbermen, fishermen, adventurers, and Indians over an area of 300,000 square miles. "Here I practiced not only medicine but was called upon to do such duties as dentistry, venterinary surgery, health officer, and on occasion filling in for the embalmer. Life in those days was a hardship for all, especially pioneering doctors. A sick call up the creek would take one or two days on horseback in the summer; dog team and sled in the winter."[7] He was assisted by an Indian Shaman or Medicine Man who "chased the devil out of the sick people," acting in the capacity of a modern psychiatrist.

In 1927 Dr. Fox paid six hundred dollars for a practice above the Royal Bank chambers at the corner of Main and Hastings Streets, between "Skid Road" and "Chinatown," and has been there for fifty years. "And the office consisted of a couch, half a dozen kitchen chairs, a congoleum rug and a roll-top desk. . . . In those days during the depression I had the largest non-paying practice in British Columbia."[8]

Dr. Fox has been described as "a friend to all the world and most especially to those people of the world who do not have many friends." In 1968 he was presented with the President's Medal by the B.C. Tuberculosis-Christmas Seal Society for his "outstanding contribution to the fight against tuberculosis." The medical association has honored him as a pioneer practitioner by naming him to senior membership.[9] For his services to the country, on the hundredth anniversary of Canadian confederation 1 July 1967, Dr. Maurice Fox was awarded the Centennial Medal.

76. THIS DOCTOR VISITED ACCIDENT CASES BY HELICOPTER, Kemano-Kitimat Transmission Line, B.C., 1951-55.

Dr. Leon Komar was born in Warsaw, Poland where he completed his high school education, then studied medicine in Great Britain. After serv-

ing as a ship's doctor in the British Merchant Navy during World War II, he came to Canada. He was physician to the Royal Canadian Air Force, Medical Health Officer, and Indian Medical Officer in the Fort St. John district of British Columbia.

'WHITEHORSE' leaving DAWSON with 90 passengers
July 14th

Dr. Komar was the Medical Officer for the Alcan-Kemano Power Project. His first office was a tent pitched at "Camp 5" to which he brought a little portable x-ray machine. He planned the modern quonset-hut base hospital at Kemano, and at the peak of construction, assisted by five nurses, looked after a community of ten thousand people.[10]

77. STEAMER *WHITEHORSE*, Leaving Dawson, Y.T., with the "Travelling Dentists," Drs. Robert Franks and Irving Snider Aboard, 14 July 1926.

The earliest known Jewish dentist to practice in Vancouver was Dr. Gerald Plant. Following him, after receiving their grade school education in Vancouver, Drs. Franks and Snider graduated from Pacific Dental College, Portland in 1924. Franks is the son of Zebulon Franks, pioneer Jewish resident, and Snider, born in England, came to Vancouver via Australia in 1905 at age two. His father was a hide and fur buyer in the interior and northern British Columbia.

The young graduates headed north and discovered that there were no dentists in all of the Yukon at that time. Travelling up and down the Yukon River on paddlewheel steamboats, they carried portable dental equipment, which could be set up in two to three hours, doing all of their own laboratory work, including bridgework and dentures.[11] They practiced in the Yukon until World War II when Dr. Snider joined the armed forces. Dr. Monty Franks, a brother to Robert, continued the practice in the war years. The Franks brothers moved to Beverly Hills, California where they have practiced dentistry since. Dr. Snider continues to practice with offices in the Georgia Medical Building.

Irving Snider is also noted for his 16 mm motion-picture films and tapes, covering all aspects of life in the Yukon, which are now housed in the Yukon Archives.[12]

78. WHITEHORSE MEDICAL & SURGICAL CLINIC, Drs. Irving Ziskrout (left) and Gerry Pelletier (right), 1948-50.

Dr. Irving Ziskrout was born on a homestead at La Macaza, Quebec, spent his boyhood on his father's farm at Lipton, Saskatchewan, then worked on the trains as a "Newsy" for nine years during the depression. Returning to studies, he graduated from University of Toronto Medical School. After serving in the armed forces, Ziskrout and his classmate established this clinic at Whitehorse, Y.T., also serving Atlin, B.C.[13]

For twenty-seven years since, Dr. Ziskrout has practiced general medicine at Abbotsford in the heart of the Fraser Valley.

79. DR. JACOB I. GOROSH, Professional Chiropodist.

J. I. Gorosh, born at Riga, Latvia but trained in San Francisco and Chicago, was one of the first professional chiropodists (podiatrists) in Vancouver. A founder of the British Columbia Association of Chiropodists, he led a ten-years' struggle to have the foot specialty recognized as one of the healing arts. Known familiarly in his profession as "Daddy Gorosh" and "Papa Jack," on 15 April 1953 at its twenty-fifth anniversary celebration, Dr. Gorosh was elected to his sixteenth term as president. He also served as president and was honored as a life member of the Canadian Association of Chiropodists.[14]

Jack Gorosh, president at the time of Samuel Lodge, B'nai B'rith, the main instigator for the Jewish Community Centre, was instrumental in the planning of the centre modelled on the best community centres then operating in North America and Great Britain. He had a great interest in youth and was founder of Vancouver AZA, the B'nai B'rith youth group. Although his plans called for a centre catering to youth and athletics, in the end they were shelved by others in favor of a more "adult club." It was not to be for another thirty-five years, when a new community centre was built, that suitable athletic facilities and youth programs were instituted.[15]

80. WESTERN SCHOOL OF PHARMACY, 1524 West Sixth Avenue, Vancouver, B.C. Photo Fall Term 1931.

William Zelner, a colorful figure in Jewish and city affairs, was one of Victoria's first druggists — on Government Street in 1858.[16]

The earliest Jewish pharmacists in Vancouver were: Louis Toban of Reliable Drug Store at Broadway Avenue and Commercial Drive, who in 1926 established the chain of thirteen Toban Pharmacies — "modern apothecary shops" — in Vancouver and New Westminster;[17] Nathan Kagnoff of Bleinheim Street (at Broadway) Pharmacy; and David Brail of Brail's Pharmacy at Oak Street and Sixteenth Avenue.

This "class of 1933" had six Jewish students: Dave Berman, Sam Cook, Henry Hersog, Mike Ratner (gold medalist), Dave Solotrow, Milton Stark.

81. MICHAEL D. RATNER, Pharmacist, Knowltons Drug Store, Vancouver's Oldest Extant Pharmacy, 15 East Hastings Street. Photo 11 August 1977.

This old-time pharmacy was founded in 1902 by Edmund S. Knowlton, Chemist & Druggist. In business for seventy-five years, for the last two

decades it has been owned and operated by Michael Ratner and Alvin Ragosin. Located near the harbor and shipping companies, this became and continues to be the only pharmacy in the marine business, supplying, servicing, and certifying ships coming into British Columbia harbors. With much truth the store has used the slogan: "Through these doors walk all the peoples of the world." Mike Ratner still practices classical pharmacy, handmaking ointments, shampoos, cosmetics, and perfumes from essential chemicals and natural oils.[18]

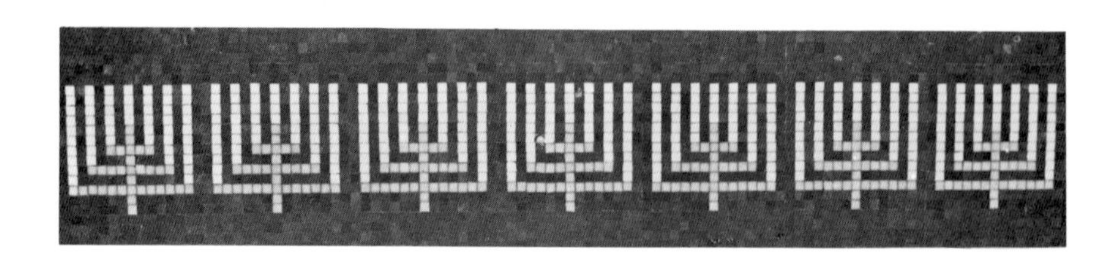

# 11

# VANCOUVER: THE PREDOMINANT COMMUNITY 1886-1977

82. PEDLAR IZIDOR WEINSTEIN WITH HORSE "BLACKIE," Vancouver Lane, 1929.

Born and educated in Rumania, the grandson of Rabbi Maryatz Wetnberger, he came to Vancouver in 1926.[1]

While Victoria was British Columbia's principal city and business centre in the nineteenth century, Vancouver was to become the predominant city of the twentieth. Vancouver was not incorporated until 6 April 1886, on completion of the transcontinental railway to the mainland coast. A handful of Jews seeing the opportunities afforded by the upstart town, destined to become Canada's great west-coast seaport, crossed the Strait of Georgia and were living here from the first days. The most notable of this group was the Oppenheimer family who, when the gold played out, came to Vancouver in 1885, and set up the first wholesale grocery business.

Up to this time, Jewish migrants to British Columbia, originating largely from the United States and from the British Empire, had already been integrated into the language, way of life, and relative affluence of Anglo-Saxon society. Starting in the 1880s several coincident events changed the direction and class of migration: beginning of the Russian *pogroms*, opening the gates of Canadian immigration to East Europeans, completion of the transcontinental railway to the Pacific Coast, Canadian government policy to fill up the empty lands of the West opened to settlement by the railways.

Most of the immigrating Jews settled in the major eastern and central cities of Montreal, Toronto, and Winnipeg, forming the largest Canadian Jewish communities. There was also a general movement westward across the continent, beginning as a trickle in the last decades of the nineteenth century and accelerating in the subsequent decades of the twentieth.[2] The new immigrants from Eastern Europe, victims of discrimination, in most cases arrived virtually penniless, with the basics of the English language still to learn. Imperfect English and a foreign accent were as much a handicap then as they are today. However, the new immigrants were an elite group with a sense of survival. They were the people who had the fortitude to leave possessions, family, and friends in the old country, the drive to travel thousands of miles, the strength to endure long journeys in the primitive transport of the day, the ambition to venture to the shores of a new, unfamiliar country. Usually too they had the attributes to succeed in a developing land of opportunity.

83. VANCOUVER SECOND-HAND STORE, Proprietor Jacob Goldberg (left), 538 Main Street, Vancouver, B.C. Photo ca. 1929.

Within a short time the East-European group grew in numbers, and by the end of World War I their influence in the Jewish community of Vancouver was predominant.[3] They brought with them several characteristics nurtured in the *ghettos* of Europe: Orthodox Hebrew religion and customs, Jewish nationalism as manifest in Zionism, penchant for democracy, passion for education, clanishness of family and community life, aggressiveness and acumen in trade conditioned from generations of hand-to-mouth living, *tzedaka* or practice of charity and justice. In the era of the "melting-pot" concept on this continent, the Jews were probably the first group to have the attitude of a truly pluralistic society. They never have regarded their citizenship in this country as antithetical to their Jewish religion, culture, or support of Jewish nationalism.

Life was hard for the early immigrant refugees from Eastern Europe. Canadian ways were almost totally alien to them. Destitute, many Jews started out in business with horse and wagon as junk pedlars (Photo 82). And the calls for "bottles, rags, and clothes" in their East-European accents reverberated throughout the neighborhood lanes of the city. Others became second-hand storekeepers (Photo 83), or artisans such as tailors and shoemakers, along the main business streets of Vancouver's early days — Water, Cordova, and Westminster (Main) — within walking distance of their homes and synagogue in the East End of town. Understandably it was these people, who had the daily contact with the general populace, that created the stereotyped image of the old-country "Jew-trader." With hard work and through mutual assistance, they eventually graduated to a better livelihood. In the 1920s and 1930s they became established as small-store owners, and a noticeable number of the retail merchandise establishments, first on Hastings and then on Granville, which had succeeded as the principal retail streets of Vancouver, were owned by members of the Jewish community.

In 1920 more than half of Vancouver's Jewish community of 250 families lived in the East End of town (Strathcona), between Gore and Raymur Avenues and between Cordova and Prior Streets, part of present-day "Chinatown." Though at the poverty level, their homes were generally clean and cheerful. By the decade of the 1930s, those beginning to ascend the economic and social ladders were establishing residences south of False Creek. A pocket of more affluent Jews lived in the classier West End.

Regardless of their financial situation, the Jewish families retained the characteristic respect for formal education. The parents and older children labored to make a good education possible for the younger children. In typical Jewish fashion, every family dreamed of having at least one doctor or lawyer. By the late 1920s and 1930s Jewish children were enrolling in the universities and entering the professions. Eventually many of these became the new leaders of the Jewish community and have made a significant mark in the overall community.

In its first two decades, the initial communal efforts of the small Jewish community of Vancouver — as with all viable Jewish communities elsewhere — were the procural of a burial ground, and the formation of religious congregations according to Jewish rites. Between 1910, when the population had grown to two hundred families, and the early 1930s when it had passed the six-hundred families mark, the structure of the Jewish community was firmly established. This period saw the founding of most of the basic organizations that form the core of the community today. Among them: B'nai B'rith (1910),[4] Hebrew Aid and Immigrant Society (1910),[5] Zionist and Social Society (1913),[6] Hebrew Free Loan Association (1915),[7] Hadassah (1920),[8] Council of Jewish Women (1924),[9] Jewish Community Chest (1924),[10] Hebrew Athletic Club (1925),[11] B'nai B'rith Women (1927),[12] Jewish Administrative Council (1932),[13] Jewish Congress (1941).[14] By 1928 a Jewish Community Centre was built as the headquarters for community organizations and events. In February 1930 a regular weekly Jewish community newspaper was established.

In the very first editorial Rabbi Solomon P. Wohlgelernter was moved to ask: "An organized community or a community of organizations?"[15] There was reportedly one rent-paying organization for every twelve Jewish families, and adding to that the number of organizations that met in private homes, the ratio was one for every six families.

Jews were at the forefront in social services. Faced with providing their own facilities, tailored to meet the particular problems of their immigrant group, they often took a lead that was followed later by the overall community. Thus in 1924 the Vancouver Jewish Community Chest was organized as the first central fund-raising body established by the local Jewish community. When the Vancouver Community Chest was established in 1931, the Jewish Chest became a model for and one of the founding agencies of the city-wide organization.[16] Today, the same may be said of the new Jewish Community Centre and Louis Brier Hospital, which serve the general Oakridge district.

The basic organizations established in the early decades of this century still ably fulfill the needs of the community. Some formed to serve the needs of the early immigrant community, such as the loan societies, have dissolved. Others have changed their structures to meet new challenges. New organizations have started. However, the rabbi's question is still timely forty-seven years later. Today there are forty principal organizations. Adding to that the various chapters, branches, and subdivisions there are close to one hundred individual groups serving a population of eleven thousand Jews in Metropolitan Vancouver.[17]

By the time of World War II the Jewish community, having attained an upward mobility, completely deserted the East End. The movement was first to Mount Pleasant and Fairview. The decade from 1941-51 also saw a rapid growth in the size of the Jewish community from 2800 to 5700 persons, with the population centering along the Oak Street corridor where the two major synagogues were built. With increasing affluence, and the opening up of new residential districts in the 1960s and 1970s, the population has continued to shift southward and westward, centering at Oak Street and Forty-first Avenue where a new Jewish Community Centre and Home for the Aged were built.

Contrary to suburban trends in American cities, the majority of the Jewish population of Vancouver continues to cluster near the central core. A census carried out by the Jewish Community Fund and Council in 1972 reported that the districts of Oakridge, Kerrisdale, South Cambie, Shaughnessy, and Fairview shared 56.8 percent of the population, with the greatest portion, 27 percent, in the Oakridge district.[18] Nevertheless, rapid growth of the adjoining municipalities within the Greater Vancouver Regional District, has resulted in the establishment of sizable Jewish populations in Richmond-Delta,[19] the North Shore,[20] and Burquest,[21] with their own organized Jewish community life.[22]

DECORATIVE WINDOW, by Egyptian-Jewish Artist Albert Sion, Beth Hamidrosh Bnai Jacob Synagogue, Vancouver, B.C.

# 12

## REPRESENTATIVE COMMUNITY LEADERS

84. DAVID OPPENHEIMER, "Father of Vancouver," Mayor 1888-91.

David Oppenheimer was the outstanding citizen in the city's critical formative period. Both David and Isaac were members of the 1887 City Council, Isaac becoming Chairman of the Finance Committee. Thereafter Isaac retired from municipal politics, devoting himself to their firm's numerous enterprises. The four-year term David served as mayor was one of the most constructive in Vancouver's history.

David Oppenheimer organized the water supply, built sidewalks and bridges connecting the segments of the city, operated a brick kiln, established the Lighting Co., the Street Railway Co., and the Electric Inter-

Urban Transit Co. He organized the Parks Board and donated generously of his land holdings for municipal parks and schools. He procured Stanley Park for the city. He established the city's YMCA and the Alexandra Orphanage. Serving the city without salary, he entertained public guests at his own expense, and contributed generously to civic funds.

David Oppenheimer promoted the establishment of Vancouver as Pacific terminus of the Canadian Pacific Railway, making several trips East on this mission. Eventually he deeded a third of his land holdings to ensure that the railway was brought to Vancouver. He promoted trade far and wide, establishing steamship connection between Canada and Australia.

His broad range of interests and activities included the presidency of: the Board of Trade; the Vancouver Improvement Co.; the Burrard Inlet and Pitt Meadows Canal Co.; the B.C. Dredging and Dyking Co.; the Vancouver Shipbuilding, Sealing, and Trading Co.; the B.C. Exhibition Association; the B.C. Fruit Growers Association; the B.C. Agricultural Association; the Burrard Inlet Rowing Club; and the Vancouver Club.[1]

On 31 December 1897, in his sixty-fourth year, David passed away at Vancouver "due to heart trouble" and was buried in the Hebrew cemetery at Brooklyn, N.Y.[2] He died the most highly respected and deeply beloved citizen of the time in Western Canada. Isaac left Vancouver in 1901. In 1922, in his eighty-eighth year, he died at Spokane, Washington, where his son Sidney, born in Yale 1873, and graduated from McGill in 1898, was practicing medicine.[3]

85. JUSTICE SAMUEL DAVIES SCHULTZ, First Jewish Judge in Canada, 1914.

Born in Victoria in 1865, Samuel Schultz was the grandson of Judah P. Davies. Educated in Victoria and at Osgoode Hall, after being called to the Bar of British Columbia he practiced law in Nelson, Victoria, and Vancouver. He was the first president of Vancouver B'nai B'rith. Justice Schultz was appointed a Vancouver County Court judge in 1914, being the first Jew in Canada named to the bench. In 1917 he became the first delegate from Vancouver to attend a national Zionist conference, and was elected to the National Council. That year he passed away untimely at the age of fifty-two.[4]

The first Jewish lawyer originating from the Vancouver community was Israel Rubinowitz, whose family arrived in 1892.[5] A brilliant Rhodes Scholar — who may have been the first Jewish recipient in Canada — he specialized in criminal law. He too died at an early age — forty-one — in 1923 of pneumonia.

86. SAMUEL GINTZBURGER, Leader of Reform Judaism.

Born in Switzerland in 1867, Gintzburger arrived in British Columbia in 1887, and followed the many diversified occupations of a pioneer. He first took up 160 acres of land on the site of North Vancouver City, then engaged in trading with the Indians on the West Coast of Vancouver Island. In 1888 he was occupied on seal hunting in the North Pacific and Bering Sea. He mined silver in the Kootenay, then joined the gold rush at Atlin, but without great success. By 1908 he was president of S. Gintzburger Ltd., "Real Estate, Insurance and Financial Agents," and a citizen of substantial influence.

Samuel Gintzburger was president of Congregation Emanu-El, Vancouver for many years. He was also instrumental in organizing the Vancouver Hebrew Free Loan Association, serving as president from 1915-24. He acted as a "big brother" to Jewish children referred to him by the Juvenile Court.

Gintzburger was a long-time consul of Sweden. He served as Councillor of West Vancouver Municipality. His varied interests included: Honorary Life President, Vancouver Automobile Club; B.C. Philatelic Society; Vancouver Scientific, Arts and Historical Society; and L'Alliance Française.[6]

87. RACHEL GOLDBLOOM, One-Woman Philanthropic Organization.

Rachel Goldbloom came to Canada from New York circa 1882, at the age of seventeen, when William Goldbloom met "this gorgeous girl and with his well-known way with the ladies swept her off her feet and brought her out to Fort Garry." Their daughter Nell was the first Jewish girl born in Winnipeg.

Arriving at Vancouver in the first decade of the 1900s, her home at 540 Burrard Street "just a couple hundred yards from the Pacific Ocean" became the centre of Jewish community life in Vancouver. Almost every Jewish organization of that time is said to have started in her home. She was a "one-woman philanthropic organization and did innumerable good deeds unbeknown to the vast majority of the populace — an outstanding example of true generosity and true humanity."[7]

She was honored in her lifetime when the second Vancouver chapter of Hadassah was named after her. The Rachel Goldbloom Chapter took on the project of furnishing the dispensary of the Nahalal Agricultural School in Palestine.[8] Mrs. Goldbloom died in April 1931.[9]

88. LOUISE E. MAHRER, Community and Cultural Leader of Nanaimo and Vancouver.

Louise Mahrer was the daughter of Rabbi and Mrs. Solomon Philo of

Temple Emanu-El, Victoria, who moved to Vancouver in 1884, and founded the first reform congregation Emanu-El here. She married John Mahrer of Nanaimo in 1893. Her interests covered a wide range of subjects in matters philosophical and musical, and her home was a centre of cultural life in Nanaimo.

The Mahrer family moved to Vancouver towards the end of World War I, and thereafter Mrs. Mahrer did a great deal for the welfare of the Jewish community. She was a founding member of Vancouver Hadassah in 1920, of Vancouver Council of Jewish Women in 1924, and of Beth Israel Sisterhood. She was first president from 1927-29 of Vancouver Auxiliary No. 77, B'nai B'rith.[10] Symbolic of the main project to which the efforts of B'nai B'rith women were devoted for many years, Louise Mahrer turned the first sod when the building of the Jewish Community Centre was undertaken in 1928.[11] The Regina Philo chapter of B'nai B'rith women in Victoria was named after her mother. Louise Mahrer died in May 1939.[12]

89. ANNE (WODLINGER) SUGARMAN, Organization Woman.

Born in 1895, the daughter of a pioneer Winnipeg family, Anne Sugarman received her college education there. In 1916 she married Ephraim R. Sugarman a prominent barrister.[13]

The Sugarmans, during their time in Vancouver from 1919-42, were leaders of Liberal Judaism in the community. In 1922 they organized the Reform Jewish Sunday School. In 1924 he drew up the constitution of the Jewish Community Chest. In the same year she became the first president of Vancouver Council of Jewish Women. Elected chairman of American Western Interstate, she was responsible for the first seeing-eye dog program in America. The Sugarmans were also prominent in formation of Congregation Beth Israel, and he presented the charter at the inaugural meeting in 1932.[14]

During World War II, while their two sons were serving overseas, Mrs. Sugarman founded and chaired for 3½ years the highly successful Red Cross "Salvage Scheme," which became the pattern duplicated in many other provinces. Anne Sugarman, along with Mrs. John T. (Nellie) McCay, for nine years were the moving force of the Vancouver Folk Festival.[15] She attended several sessions of the United Nations as an observer, and arranged for numerous famous lecturers to tour Canada on this subject. Representing women's organizations, she presented a brief on women's rights during the Canadian Bill of Rights hearings. She died at her home in Toronto in May 1973.[16]

## 90. SAMUEL ROTHSTEIN, Zionist.

Respected by everyone who knew him, and endearingly called "Uncle Sam" by young and old, Sam Rothstein in sixty years helped to plan, and sustain nearly every major institution in the organized Jewish community of Vancouver, since his arrival in 1911.

Born in a Russian village, as a youth he joined the underground left-wing Poalei Zion, where he learned to use a revolver to defend himself against the ruthless *pogroms*. One of his Zionist companions was Rocha Katznelson, later to become the wife of Israeli President Shazar. His greatest love was the Jewish National Fund and the Zionist organization, for which he worked tirelessly long before and long after there was a Jewish state. He never missed a World Zionist Congress, and was himself honored with a testimonial Negev dinner by the Jewish National Fund in 1956. He had close personal relationships with many of Israel's presidents and prime ministers, including Yitzak Ben-Zvi, Zalman Shazar, David Ben-Gurion, and Golda Meir.[17]

On his death in September 1971, the eulogy delivered by Rabbi Marvin Hier compared Sam Rothstein's work in laying the foundations of this community with that of King Solomon who built the Temple in Jerusalem:

> Although he was always looking towards the Eastern Wall and Zion, which he had built, he also succeeded in the construction of the other three walls:

The Schara Tzedeck Synagogue, the Young Judaea and Camp Hatikvah, and the Canadian Jewish Congress, which concerns itself with the welfare of Jewish life in Canada.[18]

91. ALBERT O. KOCH, "Father" of Congregation Beth Israel.

Mr. Koch came to Vancouver from the United States and founded the National Dress Co.

Beth Israel is regarded as the "child" of Albert Koch. Following Nathan Bell, he became the second president and served for fifteen years — 1933-34 and 1938-51 — encompassing the crucial periods before, during, and after the erection of the synagogue building. His zeal, leadership qualities, and financial acumen welded together a group having diverse interests, towards the common goal of a Vancouver congregation built upon the principles of Conservative Judaism. He was also instrumental in the procurement and development, along with Harry Evans, of Beth Israel Cemetery, consecrated on 28 July 1946. In 1961 he was made Honorary Life President.[19] Albert Koch passed away 16 April 1969 in his seventy-fifth year during a visit to Israel.[20]

92. JOHN REED, Talmud Torah Leader.

The career of John Reed was typical of the early Russian immigrant. Born there in 1889, he arrived at Vancouver in 1914 after discharge from the Czarist army. With a rudimentary English education acquired in night classes, he obtained such work as was available. In a short time he was in business with another Jewish immigrant, eventually starting his own successful plumbing business.

From the outset Reed became deeply involved in Jewish community affairs. In the early 1920s, when the old Schara Tzedeck Synagogue was built in the East End, with classrooms in the rear, the Vancouver Hebrew School was brought under its jurisdiction, and developed into the Talmud Torah. For ten critical years John Reed held the chairmanship of the Board of Education. Despite great financial difficulties of the small immigrant Jewish community, he struggled at the task with zealous dedication. With a strong curriculum, emphasizing use of the Hebrew language, the Vancouver Talmud Torah earned recognition for its high scholastic standards. A Junior Congregation was established to encourage full training in Jewish ritual.[21] This fostered in the young a commitment to the Orthodoxy practiced by their parents. While succeeding generations have "liberalized" the outlook of the community, the fundamental traditionalism instituted by John Reed and other pioneers has markedly influenced the tenor of the community to this day. He died in June 1975 at age eighty-six.[22]

93. LAYING THE CORNERSTONE, First Jewish Community Centre, Vancouver, B.C., 3 June 1928.

This Centre was planned and built under considerable financial difficulty at the beginning of the Great Depression. Pictured are the committee

responsible for bringing the project to fulfillment (left to right): Julius B. Jaffe, building chairman; Albert G. Hirschberg; and Max M. Grossman.[23] In 1910 Dr. Hirschberg was the first registered optometrist in Vancouver.

94. JOSHUA CHECOV, Labor Zionist, U.S.S.R. Passport Photo when He Emigrated to Canada, 1928.

In a province where labor plays a key role, it is natural that the Jewish community would have a strong Labor Zionist movement.[24] The Labor Zionists believe in the redemption of Zion through the ideals of collective ownership and self-labor, allowing no exploitation of man by fellow men.

Joshua Checov was born in Russia in 1890. An individualist, he was one of the community's best loved veteran workers on behalf of Jewish philanthropy. The twin pillars of his life were Judaism and Zionism. Through forty-seven years in Vancouver he was involved in every major aspect of the life of the community, but especially his beloved Labor Zionist organization — Histadrut, Habonim, and Camp Miriam. Mr.

Checov would assist every *meshulach* who came to town, driving them around in his now legendary truck, which was known far and wide in the city as belonging to "*Chaver* Checov." He probably held the all-time record for cards canvassed in appeal drives, averaging 150-200 annually.[25] One of the last surviving members of Beth Hamidrosh Synagogue, after thirty years of helping to maintain services, he was instrumental in having it continue in use as the Sephardic Congregation.

Joshua Checov passed away in January 1975 one month before the Histadrut Testimonial Dinner, which was to have honored his lifetime contribution to Israel and the cause of Jews everywhere. His life's work was summed up in the eulogy delivered by his son Louis: "He did not make history — but he was a historical figure. For by his existence he provided the continuity with the past and guide posts for the future."[26]

95. JACK DIAMOND, LL.D., Businessman, Philanthropist, and Sportsman.

Jack Diamond arrived in Canada from his native Poland in 1927 at age seventeen, "with a suitcase containing ambition, determination and good sense." While employed at his first job sweeping floors in a butcher shop, he spent the evenings at night school learning English. Within thirteen years he was owner of Pacific Meat Co., Western Canada's largest meat-packing plant, became B.C. advisor to the Meat Board of the Wartime Prices and Trade Board, and organizer of the B.C. Livestock Association.

Mr. Diamond's philanthropic activities in the Jewish and general communities are prolific involving fund-raising for numerous health, welfare, and educational institutions.[27] For over thirty years he has served Congregation Schara Tzedeck as chairman of the Cemetery Board, Building Committee, and other functions.[28] He was chairman of the Special Events Committee British Empire Games, first chairman of the B.C. Centennial Committee, and honorary "Mayor" of Marpole. In 1955 he was awarded the "Good Citizen of the Year" medal by the Native Sons of British Columbia, the first Vancouver Jewish recipient since inception of the award in 1922.[29]

In 1967 Mr. Diamond was appointed to the Board of Governors, in 1974 awarded an honorary Doctor of Laws degree,[30] and in 1976 installed as Chancellor of Simon Fraser University.[31]

A leading race-horse breeder and supporter of Vancouver's Exhibition Park racetrack, Jack Diamond was named by the Jockey Club of Canada "Man of the Year" in Canadian thoroughbred racing for 1976, the second recipient of the Sovereign Award — the first being E. P. Taylor.[32]

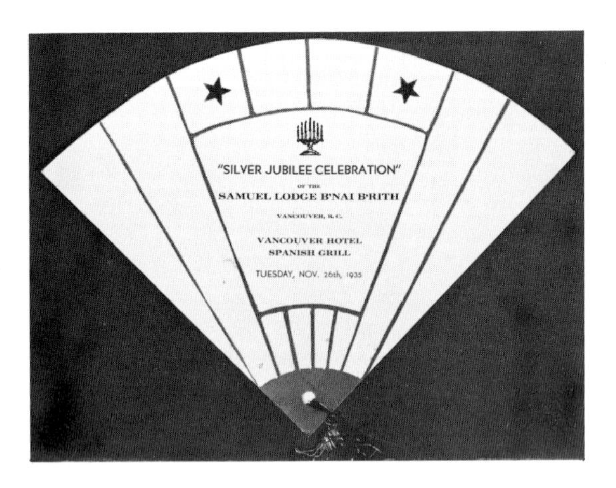


MENU, "Silver Jubilee Celebration," Samuel Lodge B'nai B'rith, Vancouver Hotel Spanish Grill, 26 November 1935.

# 13

## VANCOUVER: THE ORGANIZED COMMUNITY

96. HEBREW AID AND IMMIGRANT SOCIETY, Vancouver, B.C. Photo Picnic, 1910.

From the beginning of large-scale immigration, the Jewish people have acquired the reputation of *tzedaka*, that is "taking care of their own." The Hebrew Aid Society was one of the earliest institutions in Vancouver, assisting needy immigrants passing through the port or arriving to stay in the community, with money, food, clothes, and shelter. It also provided services to local homes, old folks' homes, hospitals, orphanages, and to inmates of asylums and penitentiaries.[1] The welfare work of this society eventually amalgamated with later organizations, such as the Jewish Community Chest[2] and the Jewish Family Welfare Bureau.

97. B'NAI B'RITH SAMUEL LODGE No. 668, First Installation Banquet, Vancouver, B.C., July 1910.

First President Samuel Schultz is seated just left of the *Menorah*.[3]

B'nai B'rith in Vancouver was organized at a meeting in the home of

Mrs. Rachel Goldbloom in the summer of 1910, with fifty-six charter members, and became an integral part of the Jewish community.

Samuel (now Vancouver) Lodge was named in memory of the deceased son of Solomon Weaver, who was one of the earliest Jewish residents in Vancouver, and a prime mover in formation of the lodge. Mr. Weaver also served as first president of the Reform congregation, Temple Emanu-El of Vancouver.[4]

98. ZIONIST AND SOCIAL SOCIETY, Meeting, Vancouver, B.C., ca. 1914.

Although Zionist activity in Vancouver has been documented as early as 1903, the first Zionist Society was organized in October 1913 with Meyer Reifman president, and granted a charter by the Federation of Zionist Societies of Canada on 10 December 1913.[5]

Since the Jewish community of Vancouver grew up in the same time frame as the growth of Jewish nationalism (Zionism) in Central and Eastern Europe, and the majority of the population came from the same well spring, it is not surprising that the community would be strongly Zionist motivated.

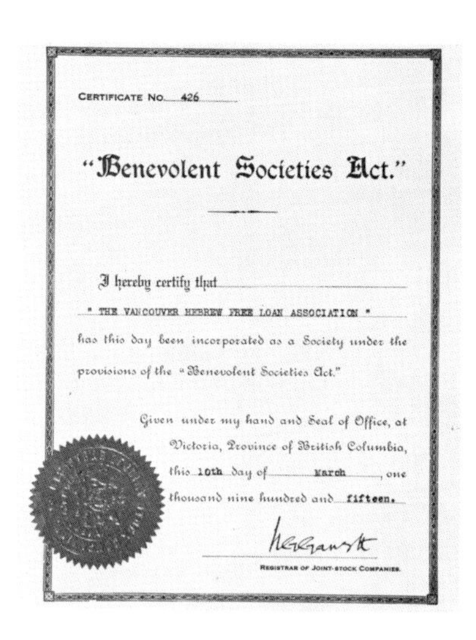

CERTIFICATE NO. 426

"Benevolent Societies Act."

I hereby certify that
" THE VANCOUVER HEBREW FREE LOAN ASSOCIATION "
has this day been incorporated as a Society under the provisions of the "Benevolent Societies Act."

Given under my hand and Seal of Office, at Victoria, Province of British Columbia, this 10th day of March, one thousand nine hundred and fifteen.

REGISTRAR OF JOINT-STOCK COMPANIES.

99. THE VANCOUVER HEBREW FREE LOAN ASSOCIATION, Incorporated 10 March 1915.

This loan society was organized by Solomon Weaver and Jacob Fleishman, with Samuel Gintzburger first president. It provided loans to the needy to a limit of fifty dollars, which were to be paid back at the rate of one dollar a week, interest free. This enabled the newcomers on arrival in Vancouver to get their start as pedlars with a horse, wagon, and business license.[6]

100. IOBB DISTRICT GRAND LODGE No. 4, Sixty-First Annual Convention, Vancouver, B.C., June 1924.

Delegates are assembled on the steps of Vancouver's Court House at a district convention of B'nai B'rith held in Canada for the first time.[7]

Founded at New York City in 1843, as a meeting ground where Jews could feel socially at home, offering varied services, and acting as an integrating force in the community, B'nai B'rith spread its roots rapidly in American soil. This organization has become unique in the annals of Jewish history owing to its mass appeal to men, women, and youth, its durability, and its anti-defamation work.[8]

101. MAY QUEEN CROWNED, at Community Chest Charity Bazaar, Vancouver, B.C., 5 May 1926.

*L to R*: Miss Dora Levi and Miss Etta Stern; the two train-bearers, Miss Rowena Herman (rear) and Miss Gertrude Chess (front) ; the Queen, Miss Etta Brotman; the page, Miss Reitza Zimmerman; Acting Mayor P. C. Gibbens crowning the queen; Miss Bessie Buckshon; and Miss Ida Poplack.

"The most successful event, both socially and financially, yet undertaken by the Jewish people of Vancouver, was the charity bazaar at Lester Court, given to augment the funds of the Jewish Community Chest."

The May Queen contest was won by Miss Etta Brotman (now Mrs. Louis LeFohn), the coronation being carried out with "pomp and ceremony," and "the procession had every appearance of a real coronation."[9]

102. THE FOUNDERS OF THE ACHDUTH ASSOCIATION, Vancouver, B.C., 1927-28.

*Top L to R:* A. Wosk, M. Korenbloom, H. Cook, E. Herbert, M. Peters.
*Bottom L to R:* S. Shine, M. Herman, W. Karasov. N. Kantor.

In 1927 Abrasha Wosk called together a small group of people to meet in his electrical and plumbing shop in front of the Avenue Theatre on Main Street near the end of the Georgia Viaduct.

Shares were sold at ten dollars each to form a unique private lending organization similar to a modern credit union, providing modest loans with dignity to struggling beginners in business.[10]

103. NEIGHBORHOOD HOUSE, Council of Jewish Women, 800 Jackson Avenue, Vancouver, B.C. Opened 15 November 1926.

Vancouver Council of Jewish Women was organized in March 1924 at the home of Mrs. A. G. (Zoe) Hirschberg. One of the first undertakings of the twenty-two charter members was the establishment of the Council Sunday School, which at its peak had 125 children attending. The school continued until 1932 when Congregation Beth Israel was formed and took over this area of work.[11]

Two years later "a dream became reality" when the Council opened its clubhouse in the East End. Mrs. Nace (Anna) Swartz was president, and Mrs. H. B. (Leah) Kahn chairman of the first House Committee. The Council House provided such activities as sewing, arts and crafts, a library, girl guide group, summer camp, and English classes, helping newcomers to become integrated into Canadian ways.[12]

The Council House was the forerunner of the Jewish Community Centre, and ceased operation when the centre opened.

104. FIRST JEWISH COMMUNITY CENTRE, Oak Street at Eleventh Avenue, Vancouver, B.C., 1928-62.

There was a long-felt need to build a "Centre" to provide headquarters for the Jewish community, offices for its organizations, meeting rooms, and athletic facilities. The first community centre was built on the instigation and financial support of Samuel Lodge B'nai B'rith, assisted by the entire community.

Phased to be built in two units, the first part was completed in the fall of 1928. With onset of the Great Depression the extension, which was to have included a gymnasium and six-hundred seat auditorium, was never

realized.[13] By the time means were available, the focus of the Jewish population had shifted southward.

Dr. J. V. "Jimmy" White was the catalyst in the drive for a new centre. After a six-year search over the Lower Mainland for a suitable site, the new Jewish Community Centre was built on Forty-first Avenue at Oak Street, dedicated before a crowd of a thousand persons on 18 November 1962.[14]

105. WELL BABY CLINIC, Council of Jewish Women, at Talmud Torah Hall, Heatley Avenue, Vancouver, B.C. Photo ca. 1931.

*L to R:* VON nurse; Mrs. M. M. (Dorothy) Grossman; VON nurse Sybil Gardiner; Dr. John R. Davies, paediatrician; Mrs. H. J. (Cecile) Allen; Mrs. A. (Alice) Lyone.

Council, on its first birthday 13 November 1927, celebrated by opening a free baby clinic at its Neighhorhood House. The clinic, chaired by Mrs.

M. H. (Eva) Brotman, operated under the supervision of Dr. F. T. Underhill, city medical health officer.[15] Dr. Davies provided his services voluntarily. The clinic, including a dental department, was in operation two days a week. Later moving to the Talmud Torah Hall, the clinic was operated by Council for eleven years, then incorporated into the Metropolitan Health Service.[16]

106. ZIONIST ORDER OF HABONIM LODGE, Vancouver, B.C. Photo 1938.

*Back L to R:* Sam Rothstein, Kiva Katznelson, Ben Shapiro, Dr. Jack Moscovich, William Nemetz, Nathan Fox, Harold Freeman, Sam Tenenbaum, Dr. Maurice Fox, Harry Toban, Dave Nemetz.

*Front L to R:* Myer Freedman, Rabbi Judah L. Zlotnik, Dr. Jacob I. Gorosh, Rabbi Solomon P. Wohlgelernter, Dave Freeman.

Many of the Jewish community leaders of the time are seen in this photograph.

1ST LADIES MIZRACHI CHAPTER IN EXECUTIVE COMMITTEE
VANCOUVER. B.C. FEB: 22ND 1941

107. FIRST LADIES MIZRACHI CHAPTER, In Executive Committee, Old Talmud Torah Hall, Heatley Avenue, Vancouver, B.C., 22 February 1941.

*Mizrachi* represents the Orthodox religious element in world Zionism. The *Mizrachi* women of Vancouver were organized at this time with Mrs. J. (Esther) Stusser, president. There have also been men's chapters.[17]

108. EDDIE CANTOR OPENS OLD FOLKS HOME, Raises Generous Sum for its Support, 1190 West Thirteenth Avenue, Vancouver, B.C., 7 July 1946.

*O cast us not off in the time of old age, forsake us not when our strength faileth.*

In 1946 the Jewish Home for the Aged of B.C. was incorporated under the auspices of the Jewish Men's Cultural Club and Ladies' Auxiliary. A sixteen-room home, formerly occupied by the Peretz School, was purchased. Prior to that time some of the aged were living "under the most depressing conditions."[18]

More than two hundred spectators jammed in front of the home for the gala opening attended by civic, provincial, and medical dignitaries when world-renowned comedian and humanitarian Eddie Cantor, accompanied by his wife Ida, fitted a shining gold key into the front door lock.

In a "celebration dinner" at the Commodore Cabaret that evening, accompanied by distinguished baritone star Jon Charles Thomas, Mr. Cantor raised ten thousand dollars towards the thirty thousand dollar cost of the home.[19]

109. NATIONAL COUNCIL OF JEWISH WOMEN, Fifth Biennial Conference, Hotel Vancouver, 26-29 May 1948.

This was the first time that Vancouver section NCJW hosted a national convention. The conference, chaired by Mrs. M. (Florence) Brown, was held at the most critical time in modern Jewish history, since on 14 May 1948 the State of Israel had been proclaimed and was fighting for its independence. The conference sent a letter to Prime Minister William Lyon Mackenzie King, asking that Canada officially recognize the state immediately. A contribution of fifteen thousand dollars was made to provide blood-bank equipment for Israel.

The conference also asked for broader immigration policies, urged fair employment laws to eliminate prejudice and protect minority groups, and passed a resolution seeking the enactment of a Canadian Bill of Rights.[20]

110. GOLDEN AGE CLUB, Garden Party at Home of Mr. and Mrs. M. Wagner, West Vancouver, B.C., June 1951.

The Jewish community's club for senior citizens was initiated in April 1951[21] under the sponsorship of Vancouver Council of Jewish Women, with Mrs. M. H. (Thelma) Ginsberg and Mrs. J. J. (Bessie) Diamond co-chairmen of geriatrics, to encourage "the recreation experiences of these people, by providing them with the opportunity to meet together and enjoy life at their own tempo." The purpose of the club "is not to do things for the aged, but to develop their own feelings of independence, self direction, and 'belonging'. . . . The goal is to keep the club democratic, giving every member an opportunity to take part, express his or her opinion, plan their own program, and wherever possible take part in the program."[22]

The Golden Age Club has been a success from the start. Now operating independently, within the program of the Jewish Community Centre, it holds regular meetings at the centre. The club takes frequent short trips to nearby places of interest as well as trips of longer duration, such as pilgrimages to Israel.[23]

you cant afford to miss it!
BAZAAR & EXPOSITION
OCTOBER 7 & 8

111. JEWISH NATIONAL FUND CANVASS, Vancouver, B.C., ca. 1952.

*L to R:* Raymond Goodman, Ben Pawer (in car), Lloyd Taylor, Brucye Klein.

In November 1917 Lord Arthur Balfour, British Foreign Secretary, declared: "His Majesty's Government view with favour the establishment in Palestine of a national home for the Jewish people, . . ."[24]

Following Theodor Herzl's[25] words that the Jewish state would be built with "the pennies of the poor," the Jewish National Fund, led in Vancouver by Sam Rothstein, Harry Toban, and Kiva Katznelson, canvassed homes each Sunday with their traditional blue boxes.[26] After formation of the state, "mass canvasses" for the fund were instituted throughout the Jewish community.[27]

112. SECOND HADASSAH BAZAAR, Executive Members of Bazaar Committee, Vancouver, B.C., 7-8 October 1953.

*Standing L to R:* Mmes I. Lipsky, A. Narod, A. Groberman, J. White, C. Groberman, Moe Levine, L. White, M. Resnik, M. Goldberg, B. Dayson, G. Thompson, B. Shapiro, B. Panar.

*Seated L to R:* Mmes M. Levine, I. Mackoff, M. Wine, H. Panar, L. Bent, S. London.[28]

On *Purim* day in February 1912, Henrietta Szold called a meeting of forty women in New York to consider how Jewish women could work for rebuilding of the Jewish homeland.[29] Using her Hebrew name *Hadassah*, they formed an organization in honor of Queen Esther, a Jewish woman who, the story tells, rose to become Queen of Persia, and revealed herself as a daughter of her people, saving them from destruction at the hands of the despot Haman.[30]

Hadassah in Canada was founded in 1917 to aid refugees in the Middle East during World War I, and since then has established chapters in every major city from Newfoundland to British Columbia. Affiliated with the Women's International Zionist Organization (WIZO), it is the largest Jewish women's organization in the world. Hadassah's greatest accomplishment has been the Youth *Aliyah* movement. Begun in 1933 with Hitler's rise to power, it has rescued thousands of children, placing them in schools, settlements, and children's villages in Israel.[31]

In 1920 Vancouver's first Hadassah, the Lillian Freiman Chapter, was organized with Mrs. J. B. (Augusta) Jaffe, president.[32] The annual Vancouver Hadassah Bazaar, first held at Seaforth Armoury in 1952,[33] and moved to Exhibition Park in 1958,[34] has become the largest event of its kind in Metropolitan Vancouver and a city-wide tradition.

PAST PRESIDENTS
JEWISH COMMUNITY COUNCIL

113. JEWISH COMMUNITY COUNCIL, Past Presidents, Vancouver, B.C. Photo February 1955.

Past presidents in attendance *L to R:* Dr. Jack Moscovich, Albert Hirschberg, Norman Brown, Paul Heller, Phil Lesser.

In August 1932 the Vancouver Jewish Administrative Council was formed as a central body encompassing the Jewish Community Chest, Hebrew Aid Society, and Jewish Community Centre.[35] Later the Council was enlarged to include representatives from all the community organizations. In 1950 a new constitution was adopted, and the name changed to Jewish Community Council.[36]

In 1955 past presidents were honored at the annual meeting, with the unveiling of mounted photographs of the eight men who had served at the head of the Council since its inception: Albert G. Hirschberg (1934, 1937), Dr. Jack Moscovich (1935-36, 1946), Robert L. Zien (1938), Sam W. Chess (1939), Phillip Lesser (1940), Harold B. Kahn (1941-45), Norman Brown (1947-48), and Paul Heller (1949-50).[37]

114. PIONEER WOMEN FORTIETH ANNIVERSARY, Western Canadian Seminar, Vancouver, B.C., November 1964.

*Back L to R:* Helen Gorbovitsky, Marion Margolis, Israel Consul and wife, Alderman Marianne Linnell, unidentified, Edith Gelmon.

*Front L to R:* Lola Hammer, Sarah Jacobson, Manya Archeck, Bertha Solman, Bernice Neuwirth.

Pioneer Women of Canada, based on the ideal of Labor Zionism, are sisters of the Working Women's Council (WWC), the association of women in Israel chiefly responsible for the equal status of women with men in wielding the pen, plough, and gun.[38]

In 1933 Pioneer Women were organized in British Columbia under the leadership of Mrs. Manya Archeck, who was president of the senior group for eighteen years.[39]

# 14

## VANCOUVER'S PIONEER JEWISH BUSINESSES

115. OPPENHEIMER BROS. GROCERY WAREHOUSE, Southeast Corner Powell Street and Columbia Avenue, Vancouver, B.C. Photo 1889.

Vancouver's first brick building was under construction when the Great Fire, which destroyed the city on 13 June 1886, passed over the foundations. Note the coal-oil street lamp. The building was fitted with iron shutters on all windows in case of another fire.

On the invitation of the Oppenheimers, the "City Hall" was moved from a tent to this building while Vancouver's first permanent City Hall was being constructed.[1] The building still stands in present-day "Gastown."

116. STORE OF ZEBULON FRANKS, 42 Water Street, Vancouver, B.C. Photo 1902.

*L to R:* Zebulon Franks; daughter, Sarah Etta; brother-in-law Joseph Blonde; Mr. Beecroft (in rear).

Open ten hours a day, six days a week, this store stocked hardware, stoves, guns, and every imaginable article — from bucksaws to boots — needed by logger, fisherman, miner, and trapper.[2] The business was carried on by son David Franks, until his death in 1966, as Y. Franks Appliances Ltd.,[3] 626 Seymour Street. The initial Y. derived from Yetta, wife of Zebulon Franks.

The earliest Jewish religious services in Vancouver are said to have been held in this store.

117. VANCOUVER JUNK COMPANY, 841 Powell Street, Vancouver, B.C. Photo 1912.

Abraham Goldberg came to Vancouver from Seattle in 1902, and established a scrap iron and machinery business. The firm with "premises, which extend for some 200 yards along the Canadian Pacific Railway's main track . . . purchases all kinds of used metal and machinery, owns extensive shops and yards in which machinery can be repaired and adjusted . . . to the requirements of sawmills, mining, and similar companies. . . . The average stock carried . . . is estimated to value $300,000." The company also owned a five-acre yard for scrap iron in New Westminster.[4]

118. PITHER & LEISER, Ltd., Wholesale Liquor Dealers, 185 Water Street, Vancouver, B.C. Photo 1912.

This firm was one of the early businesses established at Victoria, in 1858. In 1893 Max Leiser bought an interest in the company, which then traded under this name. "The firm of Pither and Leiser has grown to be one of the most important in the Province, and their importations of wines, liquors, and cigars from the principal markets of the world are extremely comprehensive."

In 1900 they established a branch at Vancouver in a "modern" three-storey building. "The offices are decorated with native cedar and are equipped on the same lavish scale as is the parent house."[5] The building stands in present-day "Gastown."

119. "THE HUB," First Men's Wear Store in Vancouver, 45 East Hastings Street, 1887-1973.

City archive's records show that this business, which operated for eighty-six years consecutively on Abbott, Cordova, and Hastings Streets, was established in 1887 by Karl Levy in a tent on the waterfront. In 1893 it was acquired by Abraham Grossman. Max Freeman bought the business in 1908, joined later by son-in-law Morris Saltzman. The store's neon revolving-hub sign on the seventy-five foot frontage was a Hastings Street landmark.

Mr. Freeman[6] acted as "banker" for the loggers when they came to town, leaving their "stakes" in the big safe at the rear. The store was a major clothing emporium in its day, with the largest floor area of any men's wear store in town. It carried everything from shoes to hats, with a full work-clothing department.[7]

Max and son Harold Freeman were noted workers in community affairs and on behalf of Israel.[8]

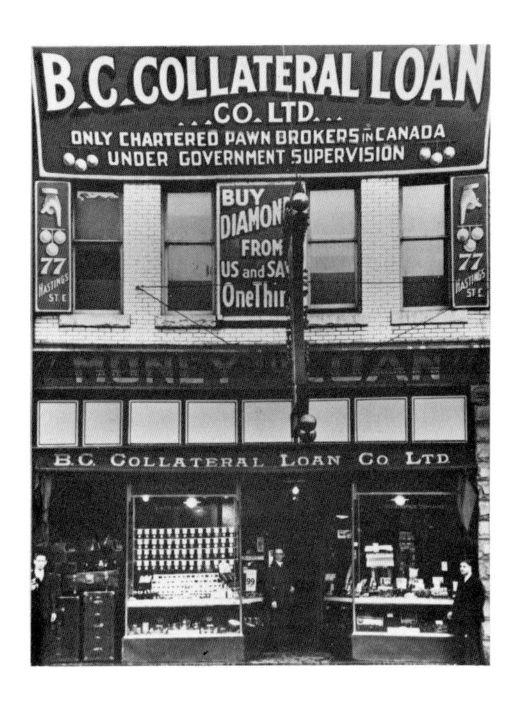


120. B.C. COLLATERAL LOAN CO. LTD., 77 East Hastings Street, Vancouver, B.C. Photo 1923.

*L to R:* Barney Glazer, Harry Evans, Jules Lipitz.

"Gastown's oldest business," founded in 1899 by Harry Evans, and located at this premises since 1909, is operated by his son Alfred.

Harry Evans was born in Europe in 1878 and settled with his family near Houston, Texas. In April 1893, at the tender age of fifteen, he and a slightly older brother ventured north to Oklahoma to participate in the famous landowners' rush. Being young and inexperienced, this bold venture was unsuccessful. Sad and wiser, the brothers returned home to continue their schooling.

In 1894 Harry Evans, hearing wonderful tales of the riches in the Pacific Northwest, decided to go north again. He wagon-trained and hiked from Texas, winding up in Montana where he worked in the Guggenheim copper mine. In 1896 he arrived in Barkerville. The lure of the Klondike was too much to resist, and in 1898 he partook in the famous gold rush over the Chilkoot Pass to Dawson City. In 1899 he decided to return to the United States.

En route south, the ship called in at Vancouver. Harry Evans disembarked — he liked what he saw and decided to stay. He had sufficient funds to establish a general store at Cordova and Carrall Streets, in what is now the heart of "Gastown." His business prospered. Harry Evans was a generous man who advanced numerous sums of money to loggers and grubstaked many a miner. So much so that this type of enterprise ushered him into the loan business, in which he was still involved until his death some fifty years later.

Harry Evans was a devoted nature and outdoors man who saw more of British Columbia than most men of his time. Every summer he took time off to explore by foot with a packsack on his back. He was well known and welcomed all through British Columbia by miners, loggers, ranchers, and farmers. It is said that he was one of the first men to walk from Vancouver to Prince George, Prince Rupert, and back. Always interested in ore discoveries, he took a correspondence course in geology. Years ahead of his time, his many findings of copper, silver, and molybdenum were not in demand.[9] Harry Evans passed away New Year's eve 1951 at age seventy-five.[10]

121. SAN FRANCISCO TAILORS & CLEANERS, 340 Abbott Street, Vancouver, B.C. Photo 1916.

*L to R:* Morris Glucksman, Joseph Snider, Ben Snider.

In 1908 Joseph Snider, a *Litvak*, established this tailoring business in Vancouver after a trip to San Francisco. Finding a competitor down the

street called Los Angeles, he named his shop San Francisco. In 1931 Snider received a patent for a multiple billing form with disposable carbons, an innovation at that time.[11]

In 1934 the premises were moved to 52 West Hastings Street, gradually changing to a pawnbroking business. Joseph Snider was active in the business until his death in 1973 at age eighty-seven.[12] Carried on by son Mitchell, it is one of the oldest Jewish-owned businesses in continuous operation in Vancouver today.

## 122. VANCOUVER UMBRELLA MANUFACTURING CO., First Umbrella Factory in Western Canada, 569 Hornby Street. Opened 1935.

Isadore Flader arrived in Toronto from Poland in 1919. He started to repair umbrellas, riding to his customers on a bicycle. Hearing that Vancouver was a rainy place and would provide a good market, he moved here in 1935. Flader, along with his wife Ida, started a family-operated umbrella manufacturing business, fabricating both frame and cover, on the ground floor of their home, with living quarters on the second storey.[13] Conditions in Vancouver proved favorable and a successful business resulted, which is operated today by his son Sam.

# 15

## EARLY RESIDENCES

123. JACOB GOLDBERG FAMILY HOME, 439 Keefer Street, Vancouver, B.C. Photo 1910.

*L to R:* Sarah, Rose, Elizabeth, Etta (mother), Anna, Jacob (father).

In the early decades of this century, most of Vancouver's Jewish people lived in simple working-class houses of this form in the East End of town, within walking distance of their shops on Cordova and Water Streets and of the synagogue at Pender Street and Heatley Avenue. Mr. Goldberg arrived from the old country in 1904.

124. JACOB IZEN HOME, 1143 Haro Street, Vancouver, B.C. Photo ca. 1918.

Mrs. Izen is standing in front of her more affluent West-End home. Jacob Izen, who came to Vancouver circa 1898, was among the earliest of a number of Jewish men in the theatre and motion-picture business. He was proprietor of the National Theatre, 58 West Hastings Street, later moving to California.

125. CHAIM LEIB FREEDMAN HOME, 123 East Fifth Avenue, Vancouver, B.C. Photo 1919.

*Back L to R:* Myer, Rose, Sara Basha (mother).
*Front L to R:* Celia, Rae.
The stone foundation was quarried at Little Mountain.

Jewish families as they became "better off" moved south of False Creek, first to the Mount Pleasant district, but still within walking distance of the synagogue, for their Orthodox religion forbade riding on the sabbath.

126. SYLVIA COURT, First Highrise on English Bay, 1154 Gilford Street, Vancouver, B.C. Photo shortly after construction in 1912.

The boom of the period brought to Vancouver's West End its first residential highrise — eight storeys above ground — setting the stage for the most intensively-developed apartment district in Canada. The "brain-child" of Abraham David Goldstein, called "Goldie" by everyone, he named the building after his "little girl Sylvia" (Mrs. H. Ablowitz).[1]

Designed by Seattle architect W. P. White, it is an excellent example of Edwardian architecture, and has recently been designated a heritage building by Vancouver City Council.[2]

127. SAMUEL SUSSEL FARMHOUSE, 10537 McSween Road, Chilliwhack, B.C. Photo June 1976.

This turn-of-the-century Gothic-revival clapboard dwelling with pointed gables, bay window, and verandah has been the home of the Sussel family for thirty-six years.

Elizabeth (left) was born in the town of Chilliwack, the daughter of Henry Brown a radiologist there.

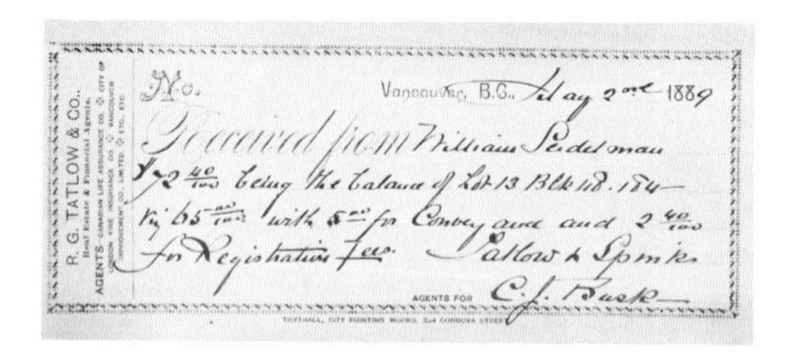

R. G. TATLOW & CO.,
Real Estate & Financial Agents.
AGENTS CANADIAN LIFE ASSURANCE CO. CITY OF LONDON FIRE INSURANCE CO. VANCOUVER IMPROVEMENT CO. LIMITED ETC. ETC.

No. Vancouver, B.C., May 2nd 1889

Received from William Seidelman
$72 40/100 being the balance of Lot 13 Blk 18. 184
viz 65 00/100 with 5 00 for Conveyance and 2 40/100
for Registration Fees. Tatlow & Spinks

AGENTS FOR C. J. Buck

TRYTHALL, CITY PRINTING WORKS, 324 CORDOVA STREET

RECEIPT, Issued to William Seidelman, for PURCHASE OF LOT at Cedar Cove, Vancouver, B.C., 2 May 1889.

# 16

## VANCOUVER: THE TRADITIONAL COMMUNITY

There is reference to Jewish religious observance as early as 1887, the year that Zebulon Franks came to Vancouver from Russia. A brilliant, well-educated man, he is regarded as the first responsible leader of the Orthodox element. The earliest Orthdox services are said to have been held in his home and store (Photo 116) on Water Street. The first *Sefer Torah* was sent out in 1888 or 89.[1]

Before the Jewish residents had a synagogue, services were held in rented halls. The first documented public Jewish service held in Vancouver "The Hebrew Yom Kippur celebrated by the local synagogue or Agudace Achim Society" took place in October 1892, and was reported in the press under the headline "God's Peculiar People."[2]

On the arrival of Rabbi Solomon Philo in 1894, who had previously served the Victoria congregation, Temple Emanu-El of Vancouver was formed, and communicated with the Reform Hebrew Union College, Cincinnati. In a letter to his colleague there, Dr. Philo reported: "My congregation counts some 22 families and we held services in a Hall as we have no Synagogue yet; but our services are strictly Reform."[3] Despite Philo's report, the congregation did not accept all the tenets of Reform Judaism as practiced in the United States but became rather "semi-Reform." The Astor Hotel next to Woodward's on Hastings Street served as a place of worship at first. Dr. Philo further acknowledged: "Also an Orthodox Congregation is here which was established two years ago; but now counts only 10-12 members all Russians."[4] Thus, from the beginning, a split developed between the more "Americanized" English-speaking Jews, and the new East-European immigrants who were Yiddish-speaking and strictly Orthodox.[5] And the old-country ways of their co-religionists were frankly an embarrassment to the more integrated Jews.

In 1907 the Orthodox congregation B'nai Yehudah (Sons of Israel) was established, with Zebulon Franks as president.[6] The boom years 1908-10 brought a great influx of people to Vancouver. The Jewish community grew to some hundred families, the newcomers originating mainly from Eastern Europe. Largely from old-country villages, they brought with them their folklore, their age-old attachment to the practices of Judaism, their Orthodox faith and *Ashkenazic* ritual. While the Reform group remained static in numbers and eventually had to disband, the community increasingly turned towards Orthodoxy.

Twenty-five years elapsed before the Vancouver Jewish community managed to build its first synagogue. In 1910 land was purchased by the Sons of Israel in the East End of town at Pender Street and Heatley Avenue, and in 1911-12 a small synagogue holding two hundred people was built. The semi-Reform congregation, or *Deutscher Shul*, continued to hold services in various locations such as O'Brien's Hall and the Labor Temple.[7] When the Jewish community had grown to 250 families, the Orthodox congregation was legally incorporated on 14 June 1917 and renamed Schara Tzedeck. Because the existing synagogue was too small, High Holy Day services were held in various rented halls: Orange Hall, corner of Gore Avenue and Hastings Street; Pender Hall, corner of Pender and Howe Streets; and O'Brien's Hall, corner of Hastings and Homer Streets, where later the Lechtziers had their bowling alleys.

In 1918 Nathan M. Pastinsky was engaged as *chason, mohel*, and *shokhet*, but soon assumed full rabbinical duties. A man of extraordinary talent, humanity, and a tireless worker, he served for thirty years until his death in 1948. Rabbi Pastinsky became the "personification of Vancouver Jewry," winning the deepest respect among the total Vancouver community.[8] On *Yom Kippur* 1919, when the management of the rented hall urged hurrying of the holy services for a dance to follow, Pastinsky delivered an impassioned sermon, which stirred the congregation to action on the dream of a new building large enough to hold the entire community on the High Holy Days.

Max Malit Grossman, a prominent barrister and community leader,[9] led the group that turned the "dream into reality." An energetic and able organizer, he headed the fund-raising and building committees, providing the driving force to make possible the new synagogue. Support of the entire Jewish community was drawn upon to unite under one roof on the original site. This included many of the Reform element, who suspended their own plans to build a synagogue on land purchased at Melville Street in the West End where most of this group lived. The new building, still unfurnished, was used for the High Holy Days in the fall of 1920. It was officially opened in 1921, when a procession left the nearby home of *Gabai* Ezedor Morris carrying the *Sefer Torahs*, and placed them in the splendid Holy Ark of the completed synagogue.[10] Today the congregation numbers 500 families.

The spirit of the Reform group did not die even though the plans for a synagogue were shelved. The Ladies' Auxiliary of Temple Emanu-El continued to operate a Sunday school for the children until it was taken over by the newly-formed Council of Jewish Women.[11]

With the growth of a second generation, Canadian-born and schooled, a demand again arose for the formation of a more modern congregation, without segregation of the sexes, and with greater English-speaking content, both in the formal services and in the religious school, while still retaining the basic tenets and rituals of Judaism. "A meeting to organize a new congregation with an English-speaking Rabbi" was held at the Vancouver Hebrew Athletic Club rooms on 30 September 1925 with Moses H. Brotman in the chair.[12] When the Jewish Community Centre opened in Fairview, synagogue services were held there. This led to the incorporation in November 1932 of a Conservative congregation, Beth Israel.[13] The semi-Reform group found it compatible to coalesce with the new congregation, which took over the running of a religious school. However, because of the Great Depression and war following, it was not until 1948 that the new congregation had the numbers and means to erect its own building.[14] Beth Israel today is the largest Jewish congregation in British Columbia, numbering 660 families.

In 1943 Beth Hamidrosh Bnai Jacob, a small ultra-Orthdox congregation using *Sephard* ritual, was established in Fairview by a quorum of eleven men led by A. Max Charkow, a stalwart community leader. Coming to Vancouver in 1917, Mr. Charkow was actively engaged in the early leadership of Zionism here. A devoted participant in religious life, he was a president of Congregation Schara Tzedeck and a founder of the Cemetery Board. He was particularly involved in resettlement of survivors of the holocaust.[15] The synagogue was named in honor of his father Jacob.

Rabbi Chaim B. Ginsberg was engaged to lead the congregation. A graduate of theological seminaries in Poland and Germany, who studied under the distinguished *Chofetz Chaim* of Poland, Rabbi Ginsberg was well known for his writings in the fields of Biblical and Talmudic studies. With the approach of the German invasion of Poland, he escaped with a party of twenty rabbis across Russia to Shanghai, but lost his entire family in the holocaust. Rabbi Ginsberg was a most revered man whose counsel was sought by people from every segment of the community.[16]

After World War II when a flood of newcomers converged on Metropolitan Vancouver, the population grew several fold and became much more cosmopolitan. This instigated the formation of new congregations in addition to the traditional ones.

On 23 July 1965 the Union of American Hebrew Congregations presented a charter to the Vancouver Reform Congregation.[17] Eighty-two years after the original Reform congregation Emanu-El of Vancouver was organized, on 12 March 1976 Vancouver's first Jewish Reform Temple was dedicated[18] in the Point Grey district, serving 180 families.

Having met for many years in private homes, on 19 January 1973 the Sephardic Congregation was incorporated, composed of one hundred Jewish families mostly from Arabic countries. They carried on services at

Beth Hamidrosh whose original congregation had largely expired. Amalgamation of the two congregations was officially consummated on 31 March 1977. The *Sephardic* outlook is basically Orthodox, the main differences being use of Oriental melodies and Spanish poetry in services.[19] The East-European Yiddish language is generally unknown to the *Sephardim*.

In recent years new Jewish communities have organized in the Greater Vancouver Regional District. This year two congregations have been formed in the fast-growing Municipality of Richmond: the Orthodox Congregation Schara Tzedeck of Richmond; and the Conservative Beth Tikvah Congregation, who have erected a synagogue in time for High Holy Day services September 1977.[20] The North Shore Jewish Community Association is holding High Holy Day services at their North Vancouver Centre. Burquest Jewish Community Association does not yet have a congregation but operates a Hebrew school. The continuing significance of the established and developing congregations on Jewish life in Vancouver is evident from a current survey by the author, which shows that forty-five percent of the Jews in Greater Vancouver have formal congregational affiliations.

128. PIONEER JEWISH CEMETERY, Fraser Street at Thirty-Seventh Avenue, Vancouver, B.C. Photo ca. 1909.

In February 1887 a large tract of land in the forest was acquired by the city for burial purposes. Located in South Vancouver on Fraser Street between Thirty-third and Forty-second Avenues, it became known as Mountain View Cemetery because of the splendid view of the North Shore Mountains. A separately-fenced area was alloted to the Jewish community on the understanding that it would pay the costs of upkeep. The first Jewish burial took place on 19 December 1892 when Otto E. Bond was interred. Apparently leaving no next-of-kin in this part of the world, his grave remains unmarked.[21]

Barney Weinrobe, an emigrant from Russia, and Sara Sarbesky from Germany, married at Montreal in January 1884. A year later their first child Nathan was born. In the winter of 1893 the family travelled by transcontinental train to settle in Vancouver. There was no fresh water on the train, and the passengers could not disembark because of Indian unrest. Three weeks after arrival, on 13 February 1893 eight-year-old Nathan died of diphtheria and was buried in Mountain View. His grave has a white sandstone marker, the oldest in the Jewish cemetery. But the Lord compensates. Three months later on 12 May 1893, at the Weinrobe home on Princess (now East Pender) Street, their daughter Gertrude

became the first Jewish birth in Vancouver. Living all of her life in British Columbia, her childhood was spent in the mining towns of Cumberland and Wellington and the smelter town of Ladysmith, where her father had stores.[22] Gertrude Weinrobe, recipient of the 1971 B.C. Pioneer Centennial Medal and an Imperial Oil Pioneer, passed away in Vancouver on 9 August 1975. She was buried in the family plot at Mountain View Cemetery near the brother that she had never known.[23]

Graphic inscriptions on the large stone monuments show that death often came early in those pioneer days: Ellen, wife of F. Kline, died August 1895 aged twenty-two years; Eddie, son of J. & D. Lukov, "killed by electric car" July 1904 aged ten years; Lena Letvinoff, "first British Columbia Jewish girl graduate McGill University 1911," died from "galloping consumption" June 1912 aged twenty-one years. And a long row of stones bears testimony to the great influenza epidemic of 1918-19 following World War I.

In the early years there was no organization to look after preparation of the bodies and burial according to Jewish rites. As required, a small volunteer group was hurriedly called together to deal with this matter. A Hebrew Benevolent Association began taking care of arrangements on 31 July 1909 when Abe Friedman was accidentally killed by his run-away horse.[24] In 1910 Chaim Leib Freedman arrived in Vancouver from Poland

and, appalled at the situation, immediately established a permanent Vancouver *Chevra Kadisha* to which he devoted twenty-six years as president.[25] Ever since, this society has had the care and management of all Jewish burials in the Vancouver area.

129. SCHARA TZEDECK CEMETERY, Original Gates, Southeast Marine Drive, D.G.S. 172, between Burnaby and New Westminster. Consecrated 3 November 1929.

When the Vancouver Jewish community increased to six hundred families, land was sought for a strictly Jewish cemetery as a community enterprise. This site of fourteen acres was acquired from the provincial government. The Schara Tzedeck Cemetery Board was created composed of members of the synagogue and of the *Chevra Kadisha*.

The cemetery was formally opened with the customary rites of Traditional Judaism, conducted by Rabbis S. P. Wohlgelernter and N. M. Pastinsky. A memorial stone in the centre of the grounds was unveiled by Mrs. Rachel Goldbloom.[26] On it are carved the words of Isaiah: *And death will cease forever, and the Lord God will wipe away tears from off every face.*[27]

130. FIRST SCHARA TZEDECK CHAPEL, 155 West Broadway, Vancouver, B.C. Opened 30 April 1944.

The opening of the first Jewish funeral chapel in Vancouver fulfilled a long-felt need of the community. The chapel was erected under the jurisdiction of Congregation Schara Tzedeck, with Jack Diamond chairman of the Chapel Committee. Purchase of a hearse was also made.[28] This chapel served until the current one at 3642 West Broadway was opened in June 1951.

The tenets of its constitution provide for the use of the chapel by the total Jewish community regardless of any religious affiliation.

131. FIRST PUBLIC JEWISH RELIGIOUS SERVICE IN VANCOUVER, Held in Dunn-Miller Block (left), 14-22 West Cordova Street, 1 October 1892.

Community *Yom Kippur* service was first held in the Knights of Pythias "Pythian Castle" Hall[29] located in this building, which is now part of the Army & Navy Department Store complex in present-day "Gastown."

132. B'NAI YEHUDAH (SONS OF ISRAEL), Vancouver's First Synagogue, Southeast Corner East Pender Street and Heatley Avenue, Built 1911-12.

This small wooden building, with Moorish-style round-arched windows, was typical of early Canadian synagogue architecture.

In 1920, when the Schara Tzedeck Synagogue was built on the same site, this building was moved to the back of the lot. The old building formed part of the religious complex, and the clapboard front was stuccoed over to match the new building. The first floor became a meeting hall, the second floor two classrooms,[30] and the basement contained a *mikvah*.

133. DAVID BELASOFF, First Rabbi, Sons of Israel Synagogue, Vancouver, B.C., from 1911-18.

The first Orthodox rabbi in Vancouver arrived 1911. Remaining for seven years, he helped to establish the first permanent Jewish congregation here. Rabbi Belasoff directed construction of the religious portions of the *shul*, including the *aron kodesh*, *bimah*, and *mikvah*.[31]

134. FIRST WEDDING, Sons of Israel Synagogue, 1 January 1914.

The marriage of Rose Belasoff to Mr. John Mallin was the first synagogue wedding in Vancouver.[32]

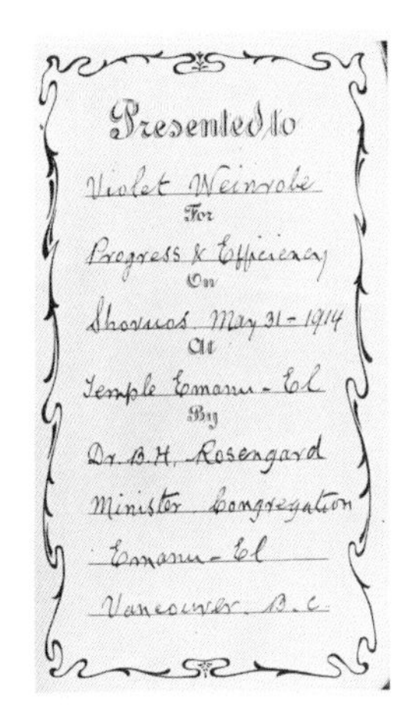

Presented to
Violet Weinrobe
For
Progress & Efficiency
On
Shavuos May 31-1914
At
Temple Emanu-El
By
Dr. B.H. Rosengard
Minister Congregation
Emanu-El
Vancouver, B.C.

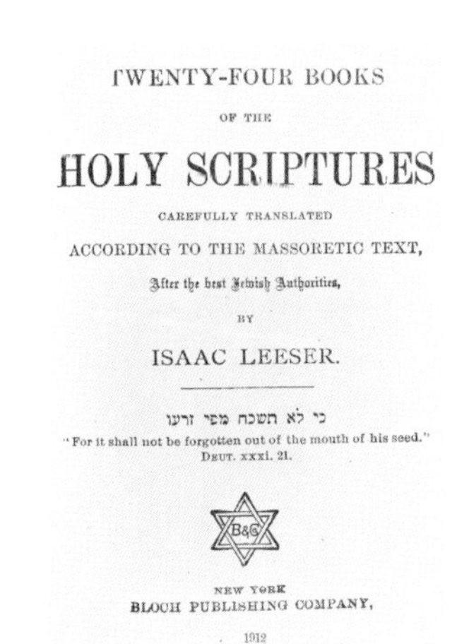

TWENTY-FOUR BOOKS
OF THE
HOLY SCRIPTURES
CAREFULLY TRANSLATED
ACCORDING TO THE MASSORETIC TEXT,
After the best Jewish Authorities,
BY
ISAAC LEESER.

כי לא תשכח מפי זרעו
"For it shall not be forgotten out of the mouth of his seed."
DEUT. xxxi. 21.

NEW YORK
BLOCH PUBLISHING COMPANY,
1912

135. TEMPLE EMANU-EL OF VANCOUVER, Presentation Page of White Bible, on Occasion of Confirmation into the Jewish Faith, 31 May 1914.

On this early date, when three girls were confirmed into the Jewish faith, the first Reform congregation brought to Vancouver a custom that was unknown to the Orthodox congregations at the time.[33] Now known as *Bas-Mitzvah* or *Bat-Torah*, it is widely practiced.

136. LAYING THE CORNERSTONE, Schara Tzedeck Synagogue, Vancouver, B.C., Spring 1920.

Rabbi N. M. Pastinsky is addressing the gathering.[34] M. M. Grossman, chairman of the Building Committee, wearing a straw hat is at far left on the platform. The original Sons of Israel Synagogue is seen in the background.

To raise funds for the building, eight cornerstones were sold that day, honoring deceased parents and grandparents. Several hundred bricks in the foundation were also sold as commemorative objects.[35]

137. FIRST SCHARA TZEDECK SYNAGOGUE, 700 East Pender Street at Heatley Avenue, Vancouver, B.C. Completed 1921.

This was the first substantial Jewish public building in Vancouver, built at a cost of $65,000. Seating six hundred persons, it was large enough to accommodate the entire congregation.[36]

The round-arched doors and windows, the wall buttresses, and Spanish-tile rooflets of Mediterranean style, were a popular idiom for synagogue architecture of the period.[37]

138. INTERIOR FIRST SCHARA TZEDECK SYNAGOGUE. Photo ca. 1927.

*Top L to R:* Ed Kravitz, Samuel Kravitz.
*Fourth Row L to R:* Yudah Tischler, Itzik Berger, Schmil Hersh (Hayit) Hyatt, Mnachem Mendel Farber, Daniel Yochlowitz.
*Third Row L to R:* Alexander (Berezofsky) Barratt, Isaac Lipovsky, Samuel Klausner, unidentified, Gershen Bobroff.
*Second Row L to R:* Shmuel Gurevitch, Leiser Rome, Maurice Kushner, Solomon Stusser, Maurice Goldberg, Benjamin Baltman.
*First Row L to R:* Abraham Levinson, David Meier Davis, Rabbi Solomon P. Wohlgelernter, David Morris.
Led by Rabbi Wohlgelernter,[38] the *Chevra Chovevi Torah* are worshipping at regular morning service.

This is a rare photograph of "fathers" of the Vancouver Jewish community, who took time off from their labors to offer morning prayer. Among them were a chicken "flicker," a *shneider*, a shoeman, shopkeepers, pedlars, and "junkmen."

139. BUILDING SECOND SCHARA TZEDECK SYNAGOGUE, 3476 Oak Street at Nineteenth Avenue, Vancouver, B.C. Photo 1947.

*And they shall make me a sanctuary, and I will dwell in the midst of them.*[39]

By the end of World War II the Jewish community had left the East End, so a new Schara Tzedeck was built on Oak Street near to the Jewish

population.[40] This photograph shows a meeting of the congregation during construction of the building.

## 140. INTERIOR SECOND SCHARA TZEDECK SYNAGOGUE.

On 25 January 1948 the new synagogue was dedicated as a memorial to the Jewish veterans of the war.[41]

When the original Schara Tzedeck was completed in 1921, the executive commissioned J. Hanbury & Co. of Vancouver to build the beautiful quarter-cut oak *aron kodesh* (centre background), where the *Torahs* are stored, and *bimah* (centre foreground) where the *Torahs* are read. These were moved to the new building and are still the centre of interest in today's synagogue.[42]

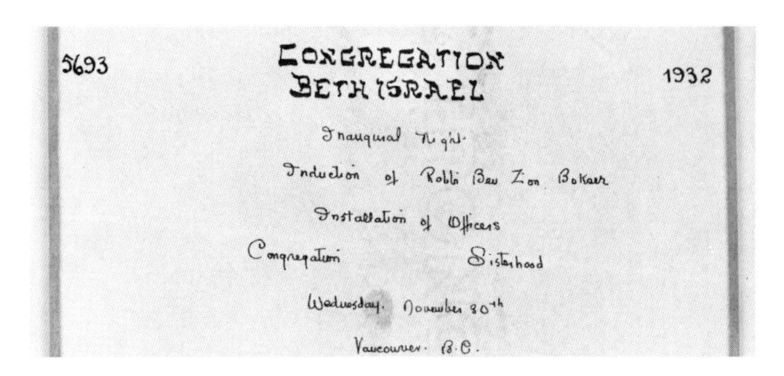

5693 CONGREGATION BETH ISRAEL 1932

Inaugural Night.

Induction of Rabbi Ben Zion Bokser

Installation of Officers

Congregation Sisterhood

Wednesday. November 30th

Vancouver. B.C.

141. CONGREGATION BETH ISRAEL, Inaugural Night, Hotel Vancouver Oval Room, 30 November 1932.

"A celebration of great importance to the Jewish community" took place this evening when Congregation Beth Israel was formally inaugurated, officers installed, and Rabbi Ben Zion Bokser inducted as spiritual leader. Rabbi Bokser said grace, and the gathering then "enjoyed a sumptuous feast."

Mr. Albert O. Koch, vice-president elect, officiated as acting chairman and offered a toast to the king. Mr. E. R. Sugarman presented the charter to the president, Mr. Nathan Bell. Mr. M. H. Brotman, secretary, proposed a toast to the Sisterhood, paying high compliments for "the active part they have taken in the Congregation." Mrs. M. (Etta) Koenigsberg, president of the Sisterhood, responded to the toast. Speakers during the evening commented on the factors in the realization of Beth Israel "as an established and recognized institution," and stressed "the vital necessity of Conservative Judaism."[43]

142. BETH ISRAEL SYNAGOGUE, 4350 Oak Street at Twenty-Seventh Avenue, Vancouver, B.C. Dedicated 11 September 1949.

This building for the Conservative congregation, designed in the modern style by Harold S. Kaplan, architect of Toronto, was publicly dedicated when Sam W. Chess,[44] building chairman, presented a key of the synagogue to Albert O. Koch, president, to indicate the building project officially concluded.[45]

143. TEMPLE SHOLOM, First Reform Synagogue in Western Canada, 4426 West Tenth Avenue, Vancouver, B.C. Dedicated 12 March 1976.

In symbolic ceremony, *Torahs* are carried into Temple Sholom's new synagogue by three generations of one family: Dr. Maurice Fox (left); grandson Joel Poll (centre); and David Poll (right), president.[46]

The scroll at the left was donated by the E. R. Sugarman family of Toronto, who were affiliated with the original Reform congregation, Emanu-El of Vancouver, and had dreamed of the day when a Reform temple would be established in Vancouver. The scroll at the right, having a rose-colored silk mantle appliqued with old tapestries in a "tree of life" design, was a Czechoslovakian *Torah* rescued from the Nazis.[47]

144. BETH HAMIDROSH BNAI JACOB, 3231 Heather Street, Vancouver, B.C. Photo 30 November 1976.

This ultra-Orthodox congregation, using *Sephard* ritual, was founded in 1943. Since 1973 it has become the home of the Sephardic Congregation.

The contemporary photograph shows story-telling time conducted by spiritual leader Gamliel Aharon at *Sephardic* Sunday school class. President Nazem J. Aboody (top) is displaying an ancient scroll of the Law, in the traditional *Sephardic* pattern, which came from Congregation Magen David in Bombay, India.

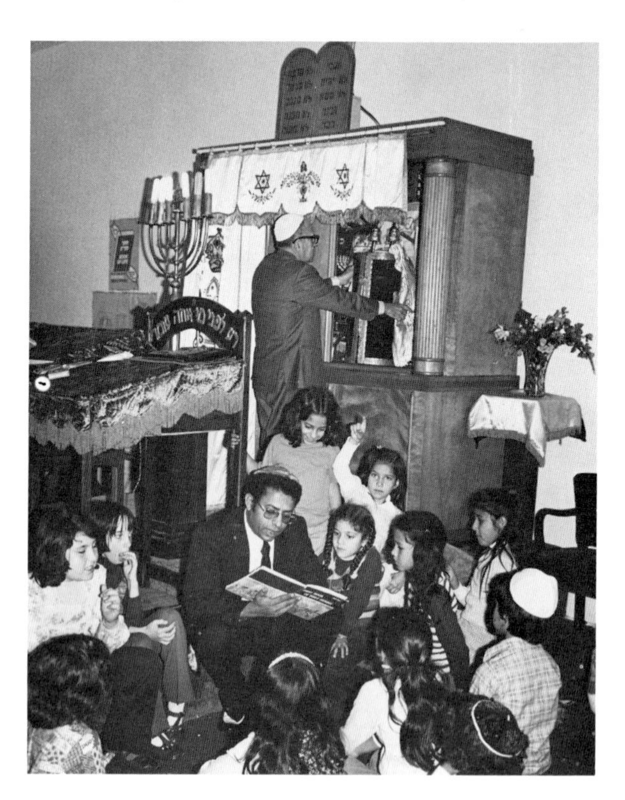

# 17

## NEWS, LIBRARIES, AND JEWISH PRESS

145. HOME TOWN PAPERS, Ben Snider at His News Stand, 335 Columbia Street, Vancouver, B.C. Photo 1923.

A Jew, W. F. Herre, was a news dealer in Victoria in 1858, and established at his place of business the colonies' first lending library of periodicals and books.[1] Ben Lichenstein, who came in 1862, operated the Occidental Cigar Store and Circulating Library on Williams Creek in the Cariboo — the "largest stock of novels ever imported on the Creek."[2] The first Jewish public library in Vancouver was organized on 30 April 1925.[3] From the inception of the Vancouver Jewish Community Centre in October 1928, a library was instituted "for our intellectual needs."[4] Having served the community with literary material of Jewish interest for half a century, the library is now housed in the new Jewish Community Centre.

The first attempt to produce an Anglo-Jewish publication occurred on 15 July 1925 when the "natal issue" of *The Vancouver Jewish Bulletin* appeared. Dr. J. I. Gorosh was editor and Mrs. I. Director, business manager. "A monthly publication devoted to the interests of the Jewish people of Vancouver," the paper was printed by Isidor Director on a small hand press at "The Printery", 337 Smythe Street. At first all the addresses had to be handwritten until an addressograph machine could be purchased. Shortly after, the premises were moved to 2355 West Broadway, where Mr. Director was a founder of the Kitsilano Chamber of Commerce, and continued in the printing business for thirty-five years.[5]

Dr. Gorosh, a man of brilliant intellect, was one of the strong voices for a Jewish community centre. The *Bulletin*, in its few years of publication, actively promoted establishment of the centre. The first editorial pledged "to work steadfastly and faithfully for the welfare of the Jewish community as a whole. . . . to be the medium through which the Jewish community will give expression to its ideals and announce its activities," and to "work for the establishment of a Community Centre, a place that will serve as a meeting ground for all factions, circles and organizations of the Jewish community."[6]

In March 1928 *Di Yiddishe Velt* magazine appeared, edited by Mordecai Jaffe, a teacher at the Vancouver Talmud Torah, and later a writer in Israel. Divided into Yiddish and English sections, this was a bold effort to establish a Jewish "literary-cultural organ" in Vancouver[7] decades ahead of its time. Only a few issues are known to have been published between 1928-35.

In October 1928 on completion of the Jewish Community Centre, the *Centre Bulletin*, a mimeographed leaflet, was published every Saturday night by volunteer labor so that it "will be in your hands every Monday morning with . . . full news concerning every Jewish activity whether held in the Centre or not."[8] The main "spirit" behind the paper was Max Grossman. By the seventh number the *Bulletin* was beginning to take itself seriously: "With each issue . . . we become more and more convinced that properly handled this little publication born in jest is destined to fill a vital need in our communal work. . . . Too long have we existed along village lines, without plan or policy. It will be our duty from week to week to point out and advocate those things our Vancouver Jewish Community should do and have."[9]

The process of evolution resulted in the appearance on 21 February 1930 of a printed tabloid, the first regularly-printed Jewish newspaper in British Columbia. The first editorial committee was headed by: E. R. Sugarman, chairman; Nace Swartz, vice-chairman; and Rabbi Solomon P. Wohlgelernter, contributing editor. The community held a contest to choose a name, the winner being *Weekly News*. But the name never stuck and the paper became *Jewish Centre News* for several months. On 9 October 1930 *The Jewish Western Bulletin* appeared on the masthead, a

*THE VANCOUVER*

# JEWISH BULLETIN

VOL. 1 JULY 15, 1925 No. 1

## EDITORIAL.

On this, the natal issue of the Vancouver Jewish Bulletin, do we pledge ourselves to work stea fast-ly and faithfully for the welfare of the Jewish community as a wh... It is our aim to be the r... through which the Jewis... munity will give expressio... ideals and announce its a... We will work for the es... ment of a Community C... place that will serve as th... ing ground for all factions and organizations of the community.

The publication of a jo... this character is always as... with a tremendous amo... work, but if this Bulletin... the community, if it wi... means of helping those o... tions whose activities are... cive to the moral, spiritual... tellectual weal of the com... the Editor will consider t... but of love.

It is our intention to cal... presentative men and wo... the community for articles... various problems confron... We will strive not to de... into a mere social gossip sh... to be a real service paper... definite place in the life of the community.

We hope that our efforts will be appreciated and the necessary support given us in order that we may go...

## RABBI BRICKNER.

By A. H. FLEISHMAN.

The Vancouver Hebrew Athletic Club, if it has done nothing else since its existence, deserves credit in sponsoring Rabbi Brickner's visit to Vancouver.

The name and fame of Dr. Brickner reached Vancouver long before his arrival...

...ner could not proceed with his speech for several minutes.

The voice of thanks extended Dr. Brickner by the British Israelites Association spoke most kindly of him, and his ad-...

# די אידישע וועלט

זשורנאל

פאר ליטעראטור, קולטור און לאקאלע ענינים.

רעדאקטאר: מרדכי יאפע.

מאי 1928 — וואנקאווער, ב.ק. — נומער דריי — ערשטער יארגאנג

### אינהאלט

## וואנקאווער אידישער קהל'שער צענטער

Vol. 1 No. 4. October 27, 1928

# Centre Bulletin

# WEEKLY NEWS

OFFICIAL ORGAN OF THE

Vancouver Jewish Community Centre

No. 1 February 21st, 1930 Vol. 1

## An Organized Community or a Community of Organizations?

Rabbi Solomon P. Wohlgelernter, Contributing Editor

There is a general problem independent of and present in endeavor of a communal nature in the work of our community, namely, the attitude of the individual to community needs. For the last three years the expansion of the community has taken such rapid progress that there is one thing, to my mind, which should be discussed by those who are interested in the development of our community. I refer to communal over-organization. I shall endeavor to suggest to the men and women who have labored so hard for the past few years in order to make our Jewish community an outstanding factor in Canadian Jewry, a solution to this problem of Vancouver.

At the present moment we have a number of organizations of a local nature which, to my mind, can be combined into one, for the benefit of the community. The waste of energy is of such great danger to the future of the community that it must be dealt with immediately if we wish to avoid the mistakes made by other communities on this continent.

In the European communities a general system of a "Kehilah" or Community Council was established, divided into various sub-committees, each one dealing with different problems of community life. Such a process of conducting the affairs of the community has helped in uniting forces of Jewry for one ultimate purpose, namely, to interest the individual member in every problem of his or her community. It included the religious, educational, philanthropic, social and financial activities of the respective communities. It also established authority and discipline in Jewish life. Those who were competent by virtue of their calling or knowledge in one of the problems, were directly interested in the solution of the problems confronting the community.

Here in this country, because Jews are not obligated to belong to the community, or to interest themselves in communal life, we have a system of volunteer members in different organizations, dealing with different problems of life. It therefore creates particular hobbies for the individual and tends to dis-unite Jewry; causes friction.

There is a sort of competition between organizations which work one against the other.

We in Vancouver are fortunate enough to be the pioneers of a growing community, and it is our duty to remove such factors and bring about unity in our work. My suggestion, therefore, is as follows:

That instead of having separate organizations, whose leaders and co-workers are interested in one or another problem of the community, that we should form the "Vaad Hair" or Board of Deputies of 24 or 30 men, elected annually by the members of the community, to conduct the affairs of our "Kehillah." This Board should be divided into various departments.

1. The Religious Department, consisting of three or five men to work for the maintenance of the Synagogue or Synagogues, and for the development of the religious life amongst Jewish people of this city. And to conduct Kosherus work of the community. Members of such a committee may be elected by the existing Synagogue and be included in the general Board of Deputies.

The Weekly News Printed by Contract by Shores Printers

*The*

# INDEPENDENT JEW

Issued every Thursday by Shores Printers Ltd.

Free Distribution to Every Jewish Home and Business in British Columbia.

Vol. 1 Vancouver, B.C. May 8th, 1930 No. 8

### UNITED PALESTINE APPEAL

#### Maurice Samuel to Reach Coast Next Week

Preparations are now complete for the reception of Mr. Maurice Samuel and the opening of The United Palestine Appeal. Mr. Samuel's itinerary will be as follows: Winnipeg May 7th, Regina May 11th, Saskatoon May 12th, Edmonton May 16th, Vancouver May 19th, Victoria May 21st, Vancouver May 26th, Winnipeg May 30th, Toronto May 31st, New York.

As will be seen, Mr. Samuel will arrive in Vancouver on Friday morning the 16th inst., and will leave on Monday the 20th by boat for Victoria. He will stay in Vancouver on his return trip all day Tuesday 21st.

#### Committees Selected

At a meeting held at the office of M. Soskin on Wednesday last the following Committees were selected: Chairman of the Appeal P. Tobin, Manager of the Appeal M. Soskin, Chairman of Banquet Committee S. W. Golden, Chairman of Publicity S. A. Goldston, Chairman of Reception Committee Dr. M. Fox.

#### Kosher Banquet To Honor Maurice Samuel

Arrangements are completed to hold a Kosher Banquet in the Community Centre on Saturday evening the 17th inst. at 7.00 p. m. with Mr. Samuel as guest of honor.

A Mass meeting will be held on Sunday the 18th inst. in the Schara Tzedek Synagogue at 3.00 p. m. at which Mr. Samuel will also speak.

#### Committee Confident

The Committee in charge feel confident that large audiences will greet Mr. Samuel on both occasions and respond in Palestine work and hold a very high place on the records for their generosity. The magnificent response they gave to the Emergency Fund proves conclusively that they have the Jewish cause at heart and are always ready to respond to the call. We fervently hope that this appeal will be no exception.

Apart from the fact that Mr. Samuel comes to us for a second visit and is one of the greatest living writers on Jewish subjects, his residence in the Holy Land, has given him a clear insight into the question of Eretz Yisrael as a Homeland for the Jews, and doubtless he will

### THE "INDEPENDENT JEW" ANNOUNCES NEW POLICY

#### Rearrangements in Plant Make Paper This Week Impossible

Owing to serious rearrangements in the plant of Shores Printers Ltd., during the last few days, there will be no regular edition of the "Independent Jew" this week.

After much deliberation the publication board has decided upon a change of policy. British Columbia Jewry can be served by a bi-monthly. The pauses being farther apart will make larger and better editions possible. The next regular edition will make its appearance on the evening of Thursday, May 16th. Thereafter and for the summer months the "Independent Jew" will be published twice a month.

### JUNIORS ARE AMBITIOUS

Don't fail to be present at the United Junior Societies' Annual Spring Frolic Dance on Wednesday night. With the proceeds the Junior Council hope to buy a bed for the Winnipeg Jewish Orphanage. The young Judaea is burdened with a debt it hopes to clear with its share while the Junior Concordia is equiping a gymnasium in the basement of the Centre. Such a united effort of all younger Vancouver Jewry deserves your support.

### THREE JEWISH STUDENTS GRANTED B. A. DEGREE

At the graduation ceremony of the U. B. C. held to-day the Bachelor of Arts degree was conferred upon Mr. Bernard Tobin with first class honors in Economics and Messrs. Harold Freeman and Harry Kostman with second class honors in a pass course.

### B'NAI B'RITH SABBATH

In accordance with the custom of The Independent Order of B'nai B'rith, Friday evening, June 20th and Saturday, June 21st have been designated as "B'nai B'rith Sabbath." While in the past no special services have been held here, the Executive Committee of the Lodge at their meeting on Tuesday last, appointed a Committee with Bro. S. A. Goldston as Chairman to arrange with Rabbi Wohlgelernter for a special service on Friday evening, June 20th. Further particulars will be announced shortly.

### DISTRICT GRAND LODGE CONVENTION

The 40th Annual Session of District Grand Lodge No. 4 will be held in San Diego, Cal., with Headquarters in the U. S. Grant Hotel, June 29th to July 1st inclusive. The actual convention will start on June 29th, but to avoid Sabbath travelling arrangements have been made to receive the guests on Friday, June 27th. According to the programme received, a lively time is assured to all delegates present in "The Air Capital of the West."

### 100 NEW MEMBERS DRIVE

Many suggestions have been made as to the best way to commemorate the 20th anniversary of the opening of Samuel Lodge. Among other suggestions was that 100 new members be enrolled. The idea was too good to be lost and it was unanimously decided that a drive to achieve name that has survived to the present day. The paper was four pages, and in the depression times cost one dollar a year or five cents a copy, the same price as a loaf of bread. In the early days the *Bulletin* had 150 paid subscribing families, and produced a fairly regular publication, for the most part through volunteer labor.[10]

For a short time in 1930 the community newspaper had a private-enterprise rival, *The Independent Jew*, published by Julius Shore and edited by S. A. Goldston. Sim Alfred Goldston was a pioneer pedagogue of Western Canada. Born in London, England in 1873, the son of a minister, he received a thorough Jewish education, as well as a general education at King's College. He came to Canada in 1892 to take charge for some years of the Jewish schools in the Hirsch Colony, Saskatchewan, improving the education, and taking a leading part in the community life of the colony.[11]

When the Vancouver Jewish Administrative Council came into existence, on 15 September 1932 it took over from the community centre publication of *The Jewish Western Bulletin*, which became the official organ of the Jewish community. John W. Herman was the first *Bulletin* Committee chairman under the Council.[12] On 7 December 1962, after thirty-two years of community control and financial support, the *Bulletin* was able to operate on its own resources, in effect becoming an independent private-enterprise endeavor.[13]

Among the notable editors and publishers of *The Jewish Western Bulletin* in the early days were S. A. Goldston, David Rome, Bernice Brown, Harry Musikansky, and Goodman Florence.[14] On 10 February 1949 Abraham J. Arnold took over as publisher and editor of the *Bulletin*,[15] succeeded on 1 August 1960 by current publisher-editor Samuel Kaplan.[16] Under these two able professional journalists, the newspaper has evolved into a first-class weekly ethnic publication, covering international as well as local events and viewpoints. In 1968 it won an Award of Excellence by the Israeli government, in competition with fifty-five Anglo-Jewish newspapers on the continent, in recognition "throughout the Jewish world for its outstanding journalism."[17] In September 1976 Samuel Kaplan was elected president of the B.C. Ethnic Press Association, comprising twenty-one ethnic publications in British Columbia.[18]

146. *THE VANCOUVER JEWISH BULLETIN*, vol. 1, no. 1, 15 July 1925.

147. *THE JEWISH WORLD*, vol. 1, no. 3, Vancouver, B.C., May 1928.

148. *CENTRE BULLETIN*, vol. 1, no. 4, Vancouver, B.C., 27 October 1928.

149. *WEEKLY NEWS*: Official Organ of the Vancouver Jewish Community Centre, vol. 1, no. 1, 21 February 1930.

150. *THE INDEPENDENT JEW*, vol. 1, no. 8, Vancouver, B.C., 8 May 1930.

151. *THE JEWISH WESTERN BULLETIN*: B.C. Centenary Edition 1858-1958, vol. XXVI, no. 26, Vancouver, B.C., 30 June 1958.

This edition marked one hundred years both of British Columbia and of Jewish settlement in this province. The cover photo shows the bronze-bust memorial by Charles Marego in Stanley Park, erected by the citizens of Vancouver to the memory of Mayor David Oppenheimer, who officially opened the park on 27 September 1888.[19] The monument was unveiled by B.C. Premier Richard McBride on 14 December 1911.[20]

# 18

## EDUCATION

152. LORD STRATHCONA SCHOOL, 500 Blocks East Pender and Keefer Streets, Vancouver, B.C. Built 1891, 97. Photo ca. 1921.

*Schoolgirls L ot R:* Bessie Buckshon,[1] Jeanette Snider, Rachel Kramer.

After incorporation of the city, the first school built by the Vancouver School District was East School, also called Oppenheimer Street School, which opened January 1887 in the Five Hundred Block Oppenheimer (now East Cordova) Street. Built of lumber from the nearby Hastings Saw Mill, it was a two-storey wooden building containing four classrooms. Heat was supplied by wood stoves; and toilets were outside.

With the rapid growth of the city, in March 1891 a new East School was opened on this site, carved out of the forest. Representing the most modern school architecture of the time, built of brick a symbol of permanence, it contained eight spacious classrooms, a hot-water heating system, and electric lighting.[2] A second larger building (seen in the photo) was completed in 1897 and is the city's oldest standing school. In 1900 it was renamed Lord Strathcona School in honor of the CPR director who had driven home the railway's last spike.[3]

This school is said to be the most cosmopolitan in the world, having as many as thirty nationalities represented at one time. Through the years it has been responsible for introducing succeeding waves of new immigrants to Canadian language and ways. Strathcona School was in the heart of the Jewish district; for three decades most of the Jewish children had their public school education in it. "After four" many also attended the nearby Hebrew school.

In 1959 a new David Oppenheimer School was built in the Fraserview district, once again honoring the name of the second Mayor of Vancouver.[4]

153. VANCOUVER TALMUD TORAH (HEBREW SCHOOL), 995 West Twenty-Seventh Avenue at Oak Street. Dedicated 8 September 1948.

There was agitation in the Jewish community, led by Jacob Fleishman, for a Hebrew school teaching day and evening classes. By 1913[5] a small

school was established in a house at 514 Heatley Avenue near the first synagogue,[6] taught by "two spinster ladies — the Rosengard sisters."[7] In 1918 a program was formalized, and the Vancouver Hebrew School was incorporated with Max M. Grossman as its first president. The finances of the school were covered by a set tuition fee to the parents of the attending children, and by annual subscriptions of the Jewish population at large.[8]

When the Schara Tzedeck Synagogue was built in 1920, arrangements were made for a combined synagogue and school. The two upstairs rooms of the old building were used for the school,[9] which eventually grew into the Vancouver Talmud Torah.[10] Among the early teachers who came to Vancouver and remained to make a sizable contribution to the community were Jacob H. Narod, Kiva Katznelson, and Joseph Youngson.[11]

With progressive movement of the Jewish population south of False Creek, in 1926 a school annex was established in Fairview, on Broadway near Cambie Street, and later moved to the Jewish Community Centre.[12] In 1943 an eleven-room house was purchased at 814 West Fourteenth Avenue as the first separate home of the Talmud Torah.[13] After World War II, under the presidency of Abe Rothstein,[14] the modern school building pictured here was dedicated, with such notable educators as Dr. S. N. Chant and Dr. G. M. Shrum present.[15] A new wing was added in 1969.[16]

Abraham Rothstein was a leading Zionist, who saw the State of Israel as an instrument for the survival of his people. However, the Talmud

Torah in Vancouver was, in larger measure, a monument to his philosophy and ideals. Recognizing that the majority of Jews would always be dwelling outside of Israel, he devoted much of his time and labors to the Hebrew School. He believed it was fundamental to the continuity of our long history, that the Jews of the *galut* be educated in the language and spirit of the *Torah*.[17]

154. VANCOUVER HEBREW SCHOOL, Executive and Teaching Staff, Spring 1927.

*Back L to R:* M. Lederman, teacher; Norman Levin; Joseph Youngson, principal; M. Kroll, teacher; Sam Klausner; Nathan J. Klausner; Isidore L. Kostman; Harry Oreck.

*Front L to R:* Abe Rothstein; Ben Margolis; Kiva Katznelson; Rabbi S. P. Wohlgelernter; John Reed; Louis Halperin, president; A. Max Charkow. The "little fellow who wriggled himself in" is Jack Klausner.

This photograph was taken at Maple Grove Park on the traditional students' holiday of *Lag B'Omer*, when both young and old relaxed from their duties for a day.[18]

155. JUDAH LEIB ZLOTNIK, Educator, in Vancouver from 1934-38.

Rabbi Zlotnik was an internationally-noted Jewish scholar and a leading Zionist. Of a rabbinic family in Poland, he organized the *Mizrachi* group there. Coming to America in 1920, he served as executive-secretary of the

Zionist Organization of Canada and director of the Talmud Torahs of Montreal. In the forefront of Jewish education and the Yiddish language, he authored many publications on these subjects.[19]

During his four years in Vancouver Rabbi Zlotnik, profound, thoughtful, stimulating, was a powerful educative and intellectual force. His deep interest in youth was a vital factor in the formation of youth groups out of which sprang many of the community's second-generation leaders. But the stage of the community at the time was too premature to take full advantage of his capacity. He left to accept the post of education director of the Jewish communities of South Africa.[20] In his last years he lived and wrote in Jerusalem.

156. FIRST PERETZ SCHOOL PTA, Vancouver, B.C. Photo 1945.

*Back L to R:* Lil Slobod, Matilda Porte, Rachel Korn, Susie Dodek, Sara Sarkin, Bernice Abramson.

*Front L to R:* Anne Wyne, Sarah Stone, Sara Rubin, Lucy Lacterman, Bunny Braverman, Galya Chud.

In 1924 the Vancouver *Muter Farein* took the lead in forming the Sholem Aleichem Folk Institute, the forerunner of the Peretz School of today.[21] They were critics of the Talmud Torah's traditionalist curriculum, and sought to establish a school to transmit their two-pronged ideology: loyalty to the Jewish people, and identification with the struggle for socialism.

The first Vancouver Peretz School opened in 1945 when a large house on Thirteenth Avenue at Birch Street was remodelled into classrooms. The school, for the "perpetuation and enrichment of Jewish life," took its name from I. L. Peretz, a foremost author and custodian of Yiddish culture.[22] In January 1962 a modern school building at 6184 Ash Street in Oakridge was dedicated "to the eternal memory of our six million martyrs."[23]

The objectives of the Peretz School are to provide a secular school teaching the children Jewish history, literature, culture, and traditions with emphasis on Yiddish, the language of East-European Jews.[24]

157. THE MENORAH CLUB OF B.C., First Annual Banquet, Vancouver, B.C., 6 May 1925.

Prior to the Menorah Club, the Henry Nathan Circle, a small coterie of professional people led by Max Grossman, Arthur Fleishman, and Samuel Petersky, met to hold discussion on an intellectual plane.[25]

In 1925 Ephraim R. Sugarman organized and became honorary president of the Menorah Society, established for the "purpose of keeping the

...3 No. 6 VANCOUVER, B. C., THURSDAY, MAY 12, 1932 $1.00 per Year

## University of British Columbia

### EXAMINATION RESULTS

WINNERS OF SCHOLARSHIPS

...AL INSTITUTION SCHOLARSHIP — Samuel L. Lipson

UNIVERSITY SCHOLARSHIP — Percy P. Saltzman

DAVID THOM SCHOLARSHIP — Harry Katznelson

Vancouver Jewry are proud to extend their hearty congratulations to the students of the Jewish faith who ...ssfully passed the recent examinations at the University of British Columbia.

It is indeed a pride and pleasure to see our Jewish youth upholding the traditions of our race, and on behalf ... Community we wish them further success.

We cannot refrain from making special mention of Percy P. Saltzman who gained two scholarships (although ... allowed to retain one), Samuel L. Lipson and Harry Katznelson, all of whom obtained the first place in their ...s. We would also specially mention Michael Lerner, M.S.A., who obtained the degree of Master of Science in Agri...re, and David A. Freeman who took first-class honors in the Bachelor of Arts Degree.

younger element of the community together and giving them advanced study on Jewish history and affairs."[26] This was the forerunner of today's Hillel Foundation and Judaic Studies on university campuses.[27]

158. SCHOLARSHIP WINNERS, University of British Columbia, May 1932.[28]

Edward Joseph Seidelman was the first known Jewish man to enter UBC, "class of Arts 1918." He died in the Battle of Passchendaele, Belgium while serving with the University of British Columbia contingent in World War I.[29] Pauline Gintzburger, B.A., M.A. "class of Arts 1919" was the first Jewish woman, and winner of the Governor General's Gold Medal.[30]

The small Vancouver Jewish community considered this its "most illustrious hour" when three of its sons became university scholarship winners. They went on to achieve distinction in their chosen fields.

Samuel Lipson (left) became head of the Civil Engineering Department UBC,[31] and president of the Association of Professional Engineers of

British Columbia.[32] He was awarded the Canadian Centennial Medal in 1967.[33]

Percy Saltzman (centre) served as Chief Regional Meteorological Officer with the Royal Canadian Air Force in World War II, and with the Canada Meteorological Service in charge of the Toronto weather office. In September 1952, as a weather broadcaster for the CBC, he was the first person seen on Canadian television, Toronto.[34] Later he gained fame as a radio and TV interviewer of many famous persons around the world.

Dr. Harry Katznelson (right), after a brilliant academic career at UBC, Washington State, Rutgers, and Cornell where he specialized in soil microbiology,[35] became a researcher and head of the Canada Agriculture Microbiology Station in Ottawa. He was also a performing violinist.

159. KAPPA THETA RHO, First Jewish Fraternity, University of British Columbia. Photo 1934.

*Back L to R:* David Westen, Sidney Evans, Milton Share, David Lesser, Jack Bell, Leslie Allen.

*Front L to R:* Charles Potter, Nathan Nemetz, Harold Lando, Sam Lipson, Herman Nemetz, Leon Holt.

HILLEL HOUSE
HILLEL HOUSE

Later, gaining international affiliation, the fraternity became Zeta Beta Tau. As an initiation stunt, candidates were required to carry a bucket down the high, steep bank to Wreck Beach and return to the top with a full bucket of water.[36]

In February 1945 Sigma Iota Pi was established at UBC as the first sorority for girls of the Jewish faith, to provide a "social, cultural and philanthropic program" on the campus.[37] In September that year it achieved international affiliation as Delta Gamma chapter of Delta Phi Epsilon with Edith Katznelson, president.[38]

160. HILLEL HOUSE, University of British Columbia Campus. Opened 5 November 1947.[39]

The B'nai B'rith Hillel Foundation sponsors a variety of services and programs on major campuses across the country, aiming to strengthen Jewish identification and to expand religious knowledge at the university level.[40] Directing its program are rabbis who serve as educators, counsellors, and pastors.[41] An early example of a seminar topic at Hillel House, conducted by Rabbi David C. Kogen, was "How can Jewish college students approach the Bible?"[42]

161. NATHANIEL THEODORE NEMETZ, Installed Chancellor of UBC, 31 August 1972.[43]

Mr. Justice Nathan Nemetz (right), new University of British Columbia Chancellor, walks in procession with His Honour Lieutenant-Governor John R. Nicholson (left) following formal installation. The same day Arthur Fouks, Q.C. (in background) ended his term as Chairman of the university's Board of Governors.[44]

Nathan Nemetz was the first person of the Jewish faith in British Columbia to hold the office of university chancellor. In a distinguished law career he gained recognition throughout Canada as an "unstuffy, liberal-minded man with a formidable reputation as a labor relations mediator." In 1963 Justice Nemetz was named B.C. Supreme Court Justice,[45] in 1968 was elevated to the Court of Appeal,[46] and in 1973 became British Columbia Supreme Court Chief Justice.[47]

# 19

## YOUTH

162. TOBAN CHILDREN, English Bay, Vancouver, B.C., 1914.

*L to R:* Harry, Dave, Louis, Alfie, Florence, Minnie.

The children of Samuel and Sarah Toban who arrived at Vancouver in 1910, becoming active, prominent members of the community: Harry and David, proprietors of Toban's Shoes and Quality Shoe Stores; Louis, pharmacist of Toban Pharmacies and Reliable Drug Store; Alfred, businessman in New Westminster; Florence (Mrs. W. Nemetz); and Minnie (Mrs. F. Toft).

163. NARROD BROTHERS, Vancouver, B.C., 1928.

*Standing L to R:* Alvin, Milton, Leonard; *Seated,* Philip.

Sons of Dr. Jacob H. Narod, well-known podiatrist of Vancouver and Victoria, who arrived in 1910 after attending a *yeshiva* in Vilna, Poland, a centre of Jewish learning. Dr. Narod was an early Hebrew teacher in Vancouver, the first cantor of Congregation Beth Israel, and conducted services at Temple Emanu-El, Victoria. Dr. Narod continued in his professional practice until he was nearly ninety years of age.[1]

The children were to become in adult life: Alvin and Milton, prominent builders, principals of Narod Construction Ltd.; Leonard, a consulting engineer; and Philip, a physician practicing in White Rock. Alvin was founding president of the new Jewish Community Centre from 1958-62.[2]

164. VANCOUVER YOUNG JUDAEANS, Executive, 1933-34.

*Back L to R:* Leon Cook, corresponding secretary; Aser Harowitz, National Fund chairman; Ruth Breger, past president girls' section; David Fouks, president; Elizabeth Hyman, vice-president; Sam Gurevitch, social chairman; Aser Rothstein, educational chairman.

*Middle L to R:* Maury Rothstein, athletic chairman; Harold Freeman, advisor; Sophie Shaffer, recording secretary; David Nemetz, leader; Myer Freedman, physical advisor; Myer Goldberg, membership chairman.

*Front L to R:* Sol "Pucky" Pelman, past president, boys' section; Harold Rome, treasurer.

Young Judaea was spearheaded at this time by Sam Rothstein, Dave Nemetz, and Rabbi Judah L. Zlotnik. Under Rabbi Zlotnik's dynamic leadership, this was regarded as the most active intellectual Jewish youth group in Canada.[3]

165. AZA CONCLAVE, Jewish Community Centre, Vancouver, B.C., 21-23 March 1940.

B'nai B'rith Youth Organization began in Vancouver when Aleph Zadik Aleph (AZA) boys' chapter No. 119 was installed on 11 November 1929.[4] There have also been two girls' chapters, Aviva and Rishona.

BBYO "strives to help its members feel at home through knowledge of their religious and cultural heritage, provide meaningful experiences in democratic self government, meet and work with friends under responsible adult guidance, and develop and practice a sense of community responsibility."[5]

166. STATE OF ISRAEL FLOAT, Wins Prize, Victoria, B.C., 24 May 1950.

*On float L to R:* Nessi Raels, Pearl Raels, Lila Israel, Stephen Bricker, Lorilee Mallek, Cyril Boas, Alan Carr.

The Jewish community of Victoria entered a float in the city's annual Victoria Day parade and won second prize. The theme was birth of the State of Israel, with children costumed to depict pioneers and newcomers to Israel.[6]

SOME JEWISH BOOKS FOR YOUR HOME LIBRARY

167. LIGHTING THE *MENORAH*, Pre-School Children, Trail, B.C., January 1955.

The Jewish community of Trail had an active youth group, ranging from pre-school to teens. In 1942 Trail Young Judaea won the national trophy for achievement, which was a significant feat for such a small community.

This traditional *Menorah*, styled after that used in the second Temple of Jerusalem, is one of the oldest symbols of Judaism. Used in their ceremonial occasions, it was also symbolic of the Judaic faith of the Trail community. When the community disbanded, in ecumenical spirit, the *Menorah* was donated to a local church.[7]

168. HABONIM DANCERS, Perform at Community *Chanukah* Celebration, Jewish Community Centre, Vancouver, B.C., 1956.

*L to R:* Rhoda Garber, Marcia Solman, Reva Rome, Bessie Segal, Cantor Abraham Deutsch, Carol Wiesenthal, Helen Wertman, Marsha Toft, Beatrice Toft.

169. JEWISH TENT CAMP, Vancouver Council of Jewish Women, North Shore. Photo ca. 1930.[8]

*Inset:* Mrs. W. (Doris) Fisher, Camp Supervisor.

The first Jewish summer camp (for girls), on a site "very suitable for tenting" at Spanish Banks, was rented for three weeks in August 1927 "to teach children how to live together, bring out the qualities of sportsmanship and provide outdoor summer recreation."[9] David Wodlinger was director of this camp. Thereafter annual summer camps were held on the North Shore at several locations including Lower Lynn Creek, Copper Cove, Deep Cove, and Fisherman's Cove. Members of the Concordia

Club were active in arranging these early camps: Harry Boyaner, Joseph Diamond, Dr. William Morris, Bill Steiner, Eph Sugarman, and Lester Weinrib. The camps soon came under the direction of the Council of Jewish Women, who provided a great deal of the volunteer help. In the early years boys and girls used the camp in alternate periods.

In April 1936, Joseph and Bessie Diamond who was president of Council at the time, searched for a permanent campsite and found "twelve wooded acres" at Crescent Beach, which they secured for a two hundred dollar cash deposit. Money was raised, construction commenced in May 1937, and the camp was dedicated in July of that year. Brothers Abe and Sam Rothstein took considerable interest in the camp, and contributed the recreation hall. Maury Rothstein was the camp's first director. The camp was truly a community endeavor. People like the Brown brothers and Chess brothers donated their business trucks on weekends to shuttle campers and goods back and forth, and businessmen of the community supplied wholesale provisions.[10]

In 1946 the Crescent Beach Camp was sold to the Zionist Organization of British Columbia to become Camp Hatikvah, the Zionist youth camp.

170. CAMP HATIKVAH, Oyama, B.C. Opened 1 July 1956.

Nestled among stately pines on the shore of Lake Kalamalka (lake of many colors), campers are housed in B.C. Camping Association approved cabins — all electrified and self-contained — in marked contrast to the early tent camps.[11]

Replacing the obsolete Crescent Beach Camp, a campsite covering forty acres in the heart of British Columbia's beautiful Okanagan Valley, was acquired by the Zionist Organization of British Columbia,[12] under the leadership of Dave Nemetz.[13] One of the best camping sites in North America, having a mean summer temperature of seventy degrees, and a fine beach front jutting out into the lake, the camp is equipped with docking facilities, a recreation centre, dining hall, shower house, guest house, athletic facilities, and Dr. William Morris Hospital. It is also the site of the senior leadership Camp Massada.[14]

171. HABONIM CAMP MIRIAM, Gabriola Island, B.C. Opened 1948. Photo Spring 1960.

The fishing is good at Camp Miriam — a fourteen-pound salmon caught with simple lure and bait by Jim Ruskin (left) of Victoria and Moshe Shak (right) of Vancouver.[15]

Habonim's youth program instills in its members a Jewish consciousness imbued with the spirit and ideals of modern Israel. Vancouver Habonim is the largest and most active in North America.[16] Camp Miriam is a vital part of the Habonim program, where its ideals are practiced by actually living them.[17]

# 20

## POLITICS

172. THE FRANKLIN BROTHERS, SELIM (left), Member of the Legislative Assembly of Vancouver Island and LUMLEY (right), Mayor of Victoria.

Selim Franklin,[1] a Liverpool Jew, "a high bred gentleman," had come to California after the discovery of gold. Opening a large store in San Francisco in 1849 he soon grew wealthy, occupying an important place in the business community, and helping to found the Chamber of Commerce there. A fire in his store, and new discoveries of gold in the Northwest, lured him to Victoria where he set up as a real estate dealer and auctioneer. Within a short time he was appointed by Governor James Douglas as the first Government Auctioneer in British Columbia.

In his first public capacity Selim Franklin became a controversial figure, and he remained so for all of his days in the colonies. In June 1859 at Victoria he conducted an auction sale of lots on the site of New Westminster, selling a reported ninety-thousand dollars worth. At the same time he gave the Governor's assurance that the proceeds from the sale would be used for streets and other local improvements. A further sale was announced for April 1860, but when Franklin arrived in New Westminster the mainland citizens raised such a tumult, apparently because of the Governor's failure to live up to the earlier promise, that he was prevented from conducting the sale.

In 1860, within two years of the first Jewish arrivals in the colony, Selim Franklin ran for the second Legislative Assembly of Vancouver Island, becoming the third Jew after Samuel Hart of Nova Scotia (1793-99) and Ezekiel Hart of Lower Canada (1807-08) to be elected to a legislature in British North America. This precipitated the first "Jewish incident" in the colony when Franklin entered the legislature to take his seat. Being British by birth he was not disqualified by the Aliens Act.[2] But he was challenged by another electee, the same Mr. Alfred Waddington who had earlier expressed his disdain at the Jewish newcomers, that he had not taken the oath of office in the prescribed form "on the true faith of a Christian." This was the same problem that Ezekiel Hart had experienced when he was expelled from the Parliament of Lower Canada. However, after days of procedural debate, and a comprehensive dissertation by Chief Justice David Cameron citing ample precedents in English law for prescribing oaths to be taken by Jews and other non-Christians, Franklin was allowed to take his seat. He was opposed to the union between Vancouver Island and the mainland Colony of British Columbia, and when that union was consummated in 1866, Franklin resigned his seat, returning to San Francisco where he served as Secretary of the Bank of California.

In 1866, the same year that Selim resigned, his older brother Lumley who had followed him to Vancouver Island, was elected the second Mayor of Victoria, the first Jewish mayor of a city in British North America. He was congratulated upon his election in a letter written in Hebrew by the Chief Rabbi of England.[3] During his term of office Lumley Franklin presided over the key public meeting at which the question of uniting the two colonies was debated, speaking in favor of the proposal. Lumley, unlike Selim, was a congenial popular man, and he received almost unanimous support for a second term. He retired, however, and never stood for public office again. Later, Lumley Franklin was to be one of the leaders of the confederation movement that brought the united Colony of British Columbia into union with Canada.[4]

173. LAST COLONIAL LEGISLATIVE COUNCIL OF BRITISH COLUMBIA, Henry Nathan, Jr. (third from right), 1870-71.

Another even more influential political figure in early Victoria was Londoner Henry Nathan, Jr., educated at University College. In 1862 he arrived at Victoria where he established a wholesale importing firm. His prolific activities ranged from Master of Victoria Lodge of the Masons to leadership of the Agricultural and Horticultural Society.

From the start Nathan was active in politics and in November 1870, at the early age of twenty-nine, he was elected Member for Victoria of the last colonial Legislative Council of British Columbia.[5] The photograph shows members of that legislature. Nathan is the only man without a beard and probably the youngest.

174. HENRY NATHAN, JR., Among First British Columbia Members of Canadian Parliament, Ottawa.

A staunch supporter and intimate friend of Sir John A. Macdonald, Nathan was influential in bringing British Columbia into confederation. When B.C. entered confederation with Canada on 20 July 1871, he was acclaimed as one of the first two M.P.'s from Victoria and among six from all of British Columbia. Thus Henry Nathan, Jr. was also the first Jew in Canada to sit in the House of Commons. He was given the honor of moving the address in reply to the speech from the throne.

These representatives only sat for one session, and in the following year Nathan was elected. While the *Colonist* reported "He has been an indefatigable worker and instrumental in obtaining many valuable concessions for the province, at the same time succeeding in securing the friendship and confidence of men of influence and power," his career in Ottawa was otherwise undistinguished. Nathan apparently was associated with the Allan interests in building of the transcontinental railway and was a Canadian Pacific Railway director.[6] He retired from public office in 1874, and in 1880 returned to his native England. Judah P. Davies stood for his seat in 1878, but was defeated by a few votes.[7]

175. CHARLES GRAHAM (left), Campaigning with Lester B. Pearson (right), Future Prime Minister of Canada, Prince George, B.C., June 1962.

Charles Graham, whose grandfather was a Scottish Jew from Glasgow,[8] came to Canada at the age of twelve, and at eighteen "rode the rods" out west. Lily Graham in 1926 escaped from a village in Russia after her father was killed in a *pogrom*. They met and married in Winnipeg. From 1954-66 the Grahams spent "the best years of our lives"[9] in Prince George where they operated a laundry, dry cleaning, and linen supply business.[10]

As leading members of the overall community of Prince George, they were active in every facet of the city's life, including service clubs, golf club, hospital, library, and Board of Trade. Mr. Graham was a Prince George alderman for six years from 1959-64,[11] president of the Industrial Development Commission, and twice a Liberal candidate for the Cariboo federal riding.

The Grahams' home was the centre of Jewish community life in Prince George. The eulogy delivered by Rabbi Marvin Hier at his funeral in April 1967 noted:

> When it came to his own faith, Charles Graham did not believe in a homogenized faith community. He thought that Jews wherever they lived should not wish to escape or avoid the historic heritage into which they were born. With equal zeal and determination he saw to it that the small Jewish community of Prince George maintained its historic heritage. He provided them with prayer books and scroll, and officiated at their services.[12]

176. PREMIER, THE HONOURABLE DAVID BARRETT (centre), Awaiting the Lieutenant-Governor to Open Fifth Session, Thirtieth Parliament of British Columbia, Victoria, 18 February 1975.

Dave Barrett was raised in the East End of Vancouver, where his father ran a produce market on Powell Street.[13] Graduating from Britannia High School, he took a Bachelor of Arts degree at Seattle University, and became a B.C. government field social worker in charge of recreation at Oakalla young offenders' unit. He received scholarships to attend St. Louis University, graduating with a Master of Social Work. After working as a staff training officer at Haney Correctional Institute, he sought elective office as the only possible instrument by which the futile correctional system could be changed. Elected to the British Columbia Legislative Assembly in 1960, Barrett was the first Jew since Henry Nathan, Jr. to hold such office.

On 30 August 1972 Barrett, as leader of the New Democratic Party,[14] achieved a landslide victory when he upset the twenty year reign of Social Credit under W. A. C. Bennett, the longest-serving premier in British Columbia history. Barrett led the first socialist government in British Columbia. He also became the first member of the Jewish faith to be elected premier of a Canadian province.[15] He was defeated in the subsequent election of 11 December 1975[16] after innovative though controversial legislation.[17]

A humane and dedicated social worker, Barrett has also served the Jewish community as: an executive-director of the Jewish Community Centre, a director of the Jewish Family Service Agency, and on the Board of Directors of Habonim Camp Miriam.

Another Jewish member of the Barrett cabinet, Norman Levi, Minister of Human Resources, was noted for his extension of social services in the province.[18]

177. MUNI SAMUEL EVERS, Mayor of New Westminster, B.C.

Born and educated in Winnipeg, Evers is the son of the late Myer Averbach who was the first principal of Winnipeg Talmud Torah, and long-time secretary of Canadian Jewish Congress, Western Region. Following discharge from the Royal Canadian Air Force in 1946, Evers settled in New Westminster, establishing Medical Arts Pharmacy. A founder of Canadian Arthritis and Rheumatism Society (CARS) in that city, he was also president of the B.C. Pharmaceutical Association.[19]

For four years Evers served as Police Commissioner of New Westminster, and in 1969 was elected Mayor. Re-elected to a fifth consecutive term,[20] he is the current incumbent. He has also served as vice-chairman, Greater Vancouver Regional District and president, Union of B.C. Municipalities. Mayor Evers won the 1974 A. H. Robins award for service to community and profession.[21]

## 178. SIMMA HOLT, Newspaperwoman and M.P.

Simma Holt was born in Vegreville, Alberta. She became interested in newspaper work during her student days at the University of Manitoba. A feature reporter for the *Vancouver Sun*, she was well known for her front-page stories on a variety of subjects including crime, police, and prison reform. Her book on the Sons of Freedom Doukhobors, published in 1964, has become a classic in its field.[22] She has won several top news awards for women.

In July 1974 Simma Holt was elected Member for Vancouver-Kingsway,[23] becoming the first woman of the Jewish faith to serve in the Parliament of Canada.

# 21

## WAR EFFORTS[1]

At the time of World War I, the small Jewish population of British Columbia, still in the early stages of forming a cohesive community, was in no position to make a significant input as a group to the war effort. Jews as individuals, of course, contributed their proportionate share by way of military and civilian service.

With the rise of Hitler to power in Central Europe in the 1930s, Vancouver Jewry, situated at the main Pacific port of Canada, unexpectedly found itself at a world crossroads, coping with a refugee problem: German, Austrian, Polish, and Czechoslovakian Jews, who had travelled across Russia in sealed cars, then by ship across the Pacific; later, refugees from Shanghai and Kobe;[2] and refugees travelling the other direction, westward from Europe to Australia and New Zealand. To assist with the influx, a Pacific branch of Canadian Jewish Congress was established, committees were set up to receive the newcomers, help those who stayed to integrate economically and socially, and to arrange the movement of people en route to other destinations.[3]

The entry of Canada into World War II in September 1939, with full mobilization, ushered in a period of intense activity. Again Vancouver Jewry, through its various organizations affiliated with the Administrative Council, played an important role. A War Efforts Committee, under the auspices of Congress, carried out numerous services at army bases throughout British Columbia: furnishing of recreation rooms and canteens, supplying of *kosher* food and Passover goods, and organizing religious services. A Service Centre was opened in the Jewish Community Centre, which offered hospitality to servicemen coming into Vancouver on short leaves, for Passover, and for the High Holy Days. And the External Welfare Fund was formed to meet emergency overseas needs.

The Jewish women's organizations were mobilized and played a substantial role in the various war-efforts programs. The Council of Jewish Women, particularly its representative Mrs. J. J. (Bessie) Diamond, assumed a vital role on the Refugee Committee. To better co-ordinate the programs, the Federated Jewish Women of Vancouver was formed in October 1939, on the instigation of Mrs. N. (Bernice) Brown and Mrs. M. M. (Dorothy) Grossman, composed of all the major women's organizations.[4] Its work consisted of: supporting the Service Centre program, providing clothing and overseas comfort, running a Red Cross workshop where bandages were rolled and sheets sewn, and performing numerous other auxiliary war services.[5]

Help of the junior organizations, who formed their own federation, was also enlisted, participating in the Red Cross program, providing hostesses and programming at the Service Centre.

These co-operative efforts of wartime resulted in a sophisticated community organization, which proved adaptable to the expanding needs of the post-war future.

179. BEN GROSSMAN, On Patrol with Model T Ford, Lybian Desert, North Africa. Photo 1916.

Grossman spent 2½ years with the British Imperial Army during World War I on motor patrol across the dangerous desert. He was invalided back to Victoria just before the armistice.

The "flivvers" were chosen for their lightness, which kept them from bogging down when driven across the unpredictable sand dunes. Condensors were installed over the radiators to prevent evaporation of the cooling water in the desert heat.[6]

180. FLIGHT-LIEUTENANT PHILIP F. WATERMAN, Royal Air Force Spitfire Pilot, Southcoast England. Photo Fall 1943.

Phil, son of beloved community worker Max "Pop" Waterman,[7] enlisted in the Royal Canadian Air Force December 1940. On fighter escort over Europe with an RAF Spitfire squadron accompanying "Flying Fortresses" of the American Eighth Air Force, he completed two tours of operations. Volunteering on Christmas day 1943 to seek German aircraft, he was shot down over Brussels, Belgium and confined in a prisoner-of-war camp in Poland until rescued by the Russian Army.[8] For his services to the Americans he was decorated with their Air Medal.[9]

Two other children of the M. M. Waterman family served in the forces during World War II: Lieutenant Matthew J. Waterman, a dentist; and Lieutenant Leah Waterman, B.Sc. in Household Economics, who interned at the Vancouver General Hospital, and went overseas with the American Medical Corps.[10]

181. RABBI CAPTAIN SAMUEL CASS, Ministering to Troops, World War II, Western Front.[11]

Samuel Cass, born at Toronto in 1907, was the first native-born Canadian rabbi to serve in Vancouver. He graduated from McGill College and the Jewish Theological Seminary of New York. Arriving in September 1933,[12] he served Congregation Beth Israel for eight years during its formative period, and was prominent in all Jewish community organizations. A member of the Vancouver General Ministerial Association, he was active in fostering inter-faith understanding.

Rabbi Cass was Chief Jewish Chaplain of the Canadian Armed Forces during World War II.[13]

182. WOMEN'S DIVISION RCAF No. 4 GROUP HEADQUARTERS, On Parade During Governor-General's Visit, Prince Rupert, B.C., Spring 1944.

Sergeant Mollie Mickelson (Klein), (top right) was secretary to the commanding officer, Group Captain Roy Foss, in charge of secret and confidential documents. This was a specially-picked operational squadron in a theatre of war at the time the Japanese occupied Attu in the Aleutian Islands. Sergeant Mickelson put in 3½ years' service during World War II at Mont-Joli, Quebec Bombing and Gunnery School, Prince Rupert, and Boundary Bay, B.C.[14]

183. HEROES DECORATED, With Distinguished Flying Cross, RCAF Sea Island Station, B.C., 22 October 1949.

Standing in front of a Lancaster bomber, Flying Officers Harold Zlotnik (left) and Tom Cooper (right), two members of the Vancouver Jewish community, were decorated by British Columbia Lieutenant-Governor C. A. Banks. Cooper, a pilot with Bomber Command, completed thirty-five missions over Germany. Zlotnik, a navigator, completed thirty-eight missions over Germany, Poland, and Czechoslovakia.[15] A brother, Sidney Zlotnik, was wounded in action on the Belgian front.[16]

184. CHARLES GORVICH (left), Presented with Meritorious Service Medal by Harry Appleton (right), Canadian Legion Fairview Branch, Vancouver, B.C., January 1955.

In June 1948 a meeting of the Jewish war veterans held at the Jewish Community Centre received a Canadian Legion charter. Lieutenant-Colonel Cecil Merritt, v.c. extended congratulations on becoming part of "the great legion movement."[17] Charles Gorvich was the founding president of this Fairview Branch No. 178.

Mr. Gorvich received the highest award of the Canadian Legion, in recognition of an "outstanding record of service" to his country, the

Legion, and the community.[18] He saw active service overseas in two world wars. In World War I he was a member of the Jewish Legion, an infantry regiment that fought under British General Sir Edmund Allenby in his conquest of Palestine.[19] In World War II Gorvich served with the Cameron Highlanders from 1939-44.

185. RALPH MOSTER, A Vancouver Boy who Gave His Life in Israel's War of Independence, 7 December 1948.

From 1943-45 Ralph Moster served with the Royal Canadian Air Force, and held the rank of sergeant pilot. In 1948 he joined the Israel Air Force. He was commander of the Negev Squadron, and rose to become Commanding Officer of Tel Aviv Airport. He was killed in a seaplane crash into Lake Kinneret (Sea of Galilee), at twenty-two years of age.[20]

Twenty-seven sons of Vancouver's Jewish community fought for Israel's defence in 1948-49.[21] A bronze plaque commemorating the men from Vancouver who fought in Israel was unveiled in May 1952 by Ben Pastinsky, in celebration of the Fourth Anniversary of the State. A party of Fairview Branch, Canadian Legion presented the colors at the affair.[22]

186. COMMANDER GERALD SANFORD LEVEY (RET.), Presenting the G. S. Levey Award to Cadet Showing Most All-Around Proficiency, Trail, B.C., 1954.

Gerald Levey at the age of twelve became a Sea Cadet in Trail. At UBC he trained in the University Naval Training Division, graduated in law, and was commissioned in 1948.

In 1951, when Princess Elizabeth (now Queen Elizabeth II) and Prince Philip toured Canada, as Executive Officer aboard H.M.C.S. *Crusader*, Lt. Levey had the honor of serving as personal aide-de-camp to the Royal Party on their tour along the British Columbia Coast.[23] He was on active service during the Korean War, was a line officer commanding his own ship, and was mentioned in dispatches.

Gerald Levey is still in the active reserve, and the naval tradition of the family is also being carried on by two of his daughters, Robin and Margo, who are also in the Navy reserve.[24]

# 22

## RECREATION

187. YOUNG MEN'S HEBREW ASSOCIATION (YMHA), Dance at Lester Court, 1024 Davie Street, Vancouver, B.C., 1910.

188. *PURIM* MASQUERADE AND BALL, O'Brien's Hall, 406 Homer Street, Vancouver, B.C., 1915.

*Purim* originated amongst the Jews of Persia. It is a holiday of frolic and merriment, having the characteristic of a spring masquerade.

189. JEWISH YOUNG ADULTS, Outing, Capilano River, North Vancouver, B.C., ca. 1917.

*Back L to R:* Myer Franks, Birdie Grossman.
*Middle L to R:* Rose Myers, Essie Raphael, Rose Izen, Leah Franks, Birdie Izen.
*Front L to R:* Sara Jacoby, Etta Koenigsberg, Dick Jacoby, Sadie Jacobs.

190. VISITING HOLLOW TREE BY HORSE AND CARRIAGE, Stanley Park, Vancouver, B.C., 1910.

Jacob Parker (front left), family, and friends.

Jacob and Pearl Parker came to Vancouver circa 1894 from Kishinev, Bessarabia, Russia. Their daughter Etta (Mrs. Charles Goldberg), born 28 July 1895, was one of the earliest Jewish births in Vancouver. She graduated from the pioneer Lord Strathcona School in 1909.[1]

191. VISITING HOLLOW TREE BY EARLY AUTOMOBILE, Stanley Park, Vancouver, B.C., 1918.

Joseph Morris and fiancé Hazel (front seat) with Mr. and Mrs. (Reva) Pinch (back seat). Hazel and Reva were sisters.

This decade saw a rapid change in transportation from the horse and buggy days to the automobile era.

Morris came to Vancouver from Russia in 1907, and was proprietor of a furniture store on Main Street. His fiancé arrived from Russia in 1912. On 9 February 1969 Joe and Hazel Morris celebrated their Golden Wedding Anniversary in Vancouver.[2]

192. SEEING VICTORIA, B'nai B'rith Victoria Lodge, 1917.

Victoria's Jewish community got together for a sightseeing tour and picnic. Julius B. Jaffe is at the wheel.

193. CONCORDIA CLUB STAG, at the Home of President A. G. Hirschberg, Vancouver, B.C., 17 February 1923.

*Back L to R:* Joseph F. Morris, Leo Mahrer, Lester Weinrib, Morris Soskin, unidentified, Harry Boyaner, Jack Rosenbaum, Dr. William Morris, Leon Gold, Jules Ablowitz, unidentified, Bill Steiner.
*Front L to R:* Phillip Lesser, Cliff Ullman, Ralph Beck, Dr. Albert Hirschberg, Joe Paul, Harry Rosenbaum, Harry Ablowitz.

This Jewish men's social club was established in September 1920 by young business and professional men of Vancouver, headed by E. R. Sugarman, "for the purpose of providing a medium of better social intercourse among the young Jewish men, and to create an atmosphere of good fellowship and understanding amongst its members." The club held regular weekly luncheons throughout the year at which well-known speakers were heard "both from within and without the community." It was "ready to help in any worthy cause, and public spirit has always been the keynote of its activities. The club has also been active in furthering social, athletic, and recreative activities in the community."[3] In truth, while the Concordia Club did do some community service, it gained the reputation as a socially exclusive group whose principal interests were the card table and the golf course.

A group having similar interests was the Montefiore Club. In May 1929 the clubs amalgamated as the Montefiore-Concordia Club.[4]

194. YOUNG JUDAEA HIKE, Hollyburn Ridge, West Vancouver, B.C., March 1927.

*Back L to R:* Sarah Nissenbaum, Matilda Nissenbaum, Hymie Goodman, Sam Cook, Bessie Davis, Max Stusser.

*Middle Back L to R:* Harold Freeman, Sophie Harowitz, Elizabeth Goldberg, Julius Shore, Bertha Breger.

*Middle Front L to R:* Rose Goldberg, Sam Feuerberg, Max Dexall, Anna Goldberg, Anne Goodman, Jack Rootman.

*Front L to R:* Myer Dexall, Sam Nesbitt, Theresa Blumberg.

"Everbody had a lovely slushy time."

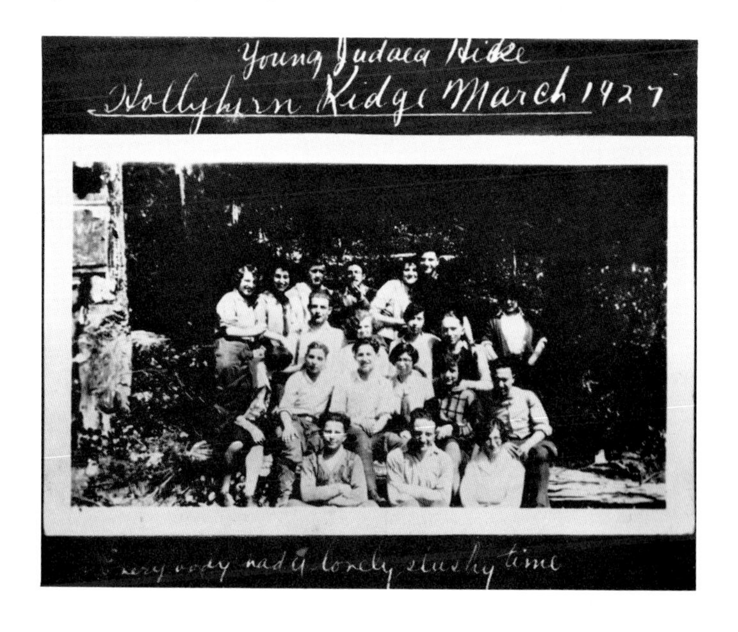

IOBB Annual Picnic Granthams Howe Sound.
June 24th 1923

Young Judaea, the Zionist youth organization, for persons between the ages of sixteen and twenty-one, was one of the most active groups in the community at this time. Meetings were held in the Zionist Hall at 456½ East Hastings Street. Operating funds were raised by having annual or semi-annual dances at the Peter Pan Ballroom on West Broadway.[5]

195. IOBB ANNUAL PICNIC, Grantham's Landing, Howe Sound, B.C., 24 June 1923.

In the small close-knit Jewish community of the decades from the 1910s through the 1930s, as in a small town, there was an interaction and camaraderie that no longer exists in today's "busy world." Such is evident in the many community picnics and other events participated in by a large section of the populace, this one under auspices of the Independent Order of B'nai B'rith.

196. DAVE CREEMER, Vancouver Diamond Jubilee B.C. Open Chess Champion, 1946-47.

Mr. Creemer was the Vancouver *Daily Province* chess editor, and president of the Jewish Chess Club of Vancouver. Prior to winning the British Columbia championship in July 1946 he had won the Manitoba championship in 1934 and the Winnipeg championship in 1937. He participated in many national and international matches, at one time defeating two international masters, the Hungarian and English champions, in simultaneous exhibitions.[6] Prior to his untimely death in 1954 at age fifty-three, he had been appointed governor of the B.C. Chess Federation.[7]

197. HARRY KOVISH, Polar Bear Champion, English Bay, Vancouver, B.C., 1 January 1950.

The champion is seen tipping his hat to the crowd as he relaxed in the water after winning his sixth consecutive championship of the Vancouver Polar Bear Swimming Club, by remaining in the icy water for twenty-eight minutes.[8] In 1951 he set the all-time mark of thirty-eight minutes.[9] Mr. Kovish "refused to turn professional preferring to devote his prowess to charitable causes." After winning his eighth championship in 1952, it was "time to declare Harry all-time champion and call it quits."[10]

# 23

## SPORTS

198. MOUNTAIN CLIMBING, Arbeiter Ring, Top of Grouse Mountain, North Vancouver, B.C., 1910.

*Standing:* J. H. Narod (second from left), Saviner brothers (third and fifth from left).
*Sitting L to R:* Joseph Snider, Joseph Narod.

The wave of immigration beginning in 1905 brought a number of intellectuals to Canada, who had been part of the socialist-cultural movement in Russia. They formed this Jewish fraternal order. "The main purpose of the organization is to get the Jewish worker away from dependence on charity and make him self-sustaining and self-reliant."[1] Critics of the Orthodox religious and educational philosophy of Traditional Judaism, they were considered radicals.

199. HEBREW ATHLETIC CLUB, Basketball Team, Vancouver, B.C., January 1926.

*Back L to R:* Sam Pelman, guard; Max Bobroff, forward; Mickey Spaner, guard.

*Front L to R:* Harry Snider, guard; Sam Izen, centre and captain; Peter Kantor, forward.

*Missing:* Dave Berman, forward.

The Hebrew Athletic Club of Vancouver was formed in 1925, with quarters at the southeast corner of Robson (No. 680) and Granville Streets above the United Cigar Store. When the Jewish Community Centre was opened, the club took the basement level hall on a permanent basis.[2]

The junior boys' basketball team in the photograph was the first to represent the club. The press reported on this "first Jewish team to be admitted to the Greater Vancouver Sunday School Athletic Association and to date has acquitted itself nobly in its division, winning most of the games played." The team was managed by Ivan Stanton and coached by Bill Katz.[3]

The club also maintained a ten-pin bowling league.

200. TEN-PIN BOWLING CHAMPIONS, Independent Order of B'nai B'rith, La Salle Recreations, Vancouver, B.C., ca. 1928.

*Back L to R:* Sam Hyman, Max Poplack, Max Beck.
*Seated L to R:* Myer Brown, Harry Woolfe.

The B'nai B'rith Athletic Association was organized in May 1925 to provide athletic activities for members of the Vancouver lodge.[4]

Jewish bowling leagues in Vancouver started after the Lechtzier brothers opened La Salle Recreations in October 1927. Both B'nai B'rith and the Hebrew Athletic Club formed leagues, which eventually amalgamated into one.[5]

201. EQUESTRIAN PHILIP BROTMAN, Vancouver Area, ca. 1930.

Phil Brotman, who first learned his horsemanship as an 1894 Wapella, Saskatchewan homesteader, was an accomplished English-style rider in

Vancouver. In those days the riding stables were on Alberni Street, with bridle trails in Stanley Park.[6]

Following David Marks and Isidore Kostman,[7] in 1923-24 Mr. Brotman was the third president of Congregation Schara Tzedeck.[8]

## 202. EARLY GOLF FOURSOME, Vancouver, B.C., 1933.

*Players L to R:* Larry Berg, Dave Franks, Alter Silverson, Harry Boyaner.

In Vancouver, golf and bowling have been the principal group sports of the Jewish community. Golf tournaments were held in the 1920s and 1930s, with competitors playing for the Harry J. Allen and I. J. "Hicky" Klein trophies.[9]

After World War II the number of Jewish golf players increased. Around 1947 some fifty joined together as a group calling themselves the Cedarcrest Club. They played and held tournaments[10] at public golf courses — principally Langara but also at Fraserview and Peace Portal. Owing to antipathy towards Jews by the private clubs, the Jewish golfers sought a club of their own.[11]

## 203. GLENEAGLES GOLF AND COUNTRY CLUB, Inaugural of First Jewish Golf Club, West Vancouver, B.C., Summer 1952.

In January 1951 a committee of Cedarcrest went out to look over property at Gleneagles near the mouth of Howe Sound. By the end of 1952 one hundred memberships at five hundred dollars each were sold, enabling purchase of the seventy-acre nine-hole course at a cost of fifty thousand dollars. The first executive included: Esmond Lando, honorary president; Dave Sears, president; and Myer Brown, first vice-president.

The Greens Committee "undertook the Herculean task of converting a cow pasture into a golf course." In the summer of 1952 the first small pan-abode clubhouse was erected[12] but was soon "bursting at the seams." A "rambling and spacious new clubhouse," with a lounge and dining room "capable of accommodating 300 people at dinner," was dedicated on 3 July 1954.[13]

Gleneagles was sold in July 1958 to become a municipal golf course. Plans were made to build a full-length eighteen-hole golf course at 9100 Steveston Highway in the Municipality of Richmond, B.C.[14] The course was built by Northern Industries Ltd. under supervision of Jack Bell. The clubhouse, designed by Architect Harald Weinreich, was built by Narod Construction Ltd. On 27 September 1959 the Richmond Country Club was "opened for the use and enjoyment of its members." The first Board of Directors was headed by: Sam Wasserman, president; Jack T. Bell, vice-president; and Dr. William Morris, secretary.[15]

Designed by A. Vernon Macan, a leading golf-course architect, Richmond is a full professional golf course in every respect. Raised greens and inverted saucers are reminiscent of famous courses in Scotland. It has hosted championship tournaments, including the B.C. Amateur and Women's PNGA (Pacific Northwest Golf Association).[16]

204. YOUNG JUDAEA SOFTBALL TEAM, Vancouver, B.C., 1933.

*Back L to R:* Jack Hersog, Sam Kalensky, Aser Rothstein, Abe Charkow, Mitch Kantor, Sam Cook, Dave Fouks, Leon Cook, "Pucky" Pelman, Sam Gurevitch.

*Front L to R:* Norman Rothstein, Maury Rothstein, Sam Rothstein, Sr. (in back), Roy Kantor (in front), Aser Rothstein, Sr., Norman Pelman.

Periodically through the years, softball teams have been organized in the Jewish community on an amateur basis.

Prior to World War II, a YMHA baseball team was organized by Dave Sears and Saul Lechtzier, strong enough to win the City Senior Softball Championship. However, after playing for a few years, the team disbanded at the outset of war.[17]

205. INTERNATIONAL SOFTBALL CHAMPIONS, Vancouver Lions Gate Lodge, Tournament of B'nai B'rith Northwest Lodges, July 1955.[18]

*Standing L to R:* Irving Grad, Sam Nep, Harry Broverman, Norman Margolis

*Front L to R:* Tommy Zabensky; Chuck Kemp; Al Jackson, captain; Sam Gordon; Dave Jackson.

*Missing:* Ed Bellas, Hy Kopelow, Norm Pawer, Lou Huberman.

206. "SILVER BOY" BOXING TOURNEY, Won by Jewish Boy, Vancouver, B.C., March 1952.

Jack Schreiber (centre) is shown with his father Max (left) and brother Harry (right) on the bicycle he won in the tournament.

This thirteen-year-old boy, who came to Vancouver with his family in 1948 from a displaced persons' camp in Germany under the Canadian Jewish Congress "Tailors Project," won the Silver Gloves Championship as the lad declared the best boxer in the junior tournament sponsored by the Irish Fusiliers, at Stanley Park Armoury.[19]

207. FREYDA BERMAN (left), of Vancouver, B.C. Wins 200-Metre Dash in Maccabiah Games, Ramat-Gan Stadium, Israel, 15 September 1957.[20]

Freyda is seen at the finish of the event where she defeated Rhoda Abel (right) of South Africa before fifty thousand spectators.

In modern times two of Vancouver's young Jewish female athletes achieved national and international status in their chosen sports.

Freyda Berman, regarded as one of the top female sprinters in Canada, discovered that she was fleet-footed at Beth Israel and B'nai B'rith picnics. At age fifteen, in an inter-high school track meet, she ran the sixty-yard dash in seven seconds flat, tying the Canadian open women's record set back in 1928 by Myrtle Cook, an all-time great of Canadian track.[21]

Patterned after the Olympics, the Maccabiah is open to Jewish athletes from all over the world. Freyda came home to Vancouver with four medals — two gold and two silver.[22]

A member of the Vancouver Olympic Club, in 1958 Freyda Berman was chosen by press and radio sportswriters as the first recipient of the "Outstanding Junior Athlete of the Year" award.[23]

208. VICKI BERNER, International Tennis Star at age Fourteen. Photo Vancouver, B.C., September 1959.[24]

At age fourteen Vicki Berner made a tennis tour of Eastern Canada and the United States, and brought back to Vancouver six singles and two doubles titles. Between 1958-61 she was four times a national juvenile and junior Canadian women's tennis champion.[25] In 1962 she won the British Columbia Junior Claycourts Open Championship, the first time for a B.C. girl. She was named to Canada's international women's tennis team,[26] and played six times at Wimbledon. Miss Berner participated in three Maccabiahs between 1961-69, and was a gold medalist.[27]

Vicki whose "court trademarks are dark glasses and famed temperament" was a member of Vancouver's Jericho Tennis Club. She turned professional in 1971.[28]

209. WILLIAM MOSCOVITZ (second from right), of Kimberley, B.C., Playing in the Canadian Curling Championships, Moncton, N.B., March 1956.

Bill Moscovitz started curling in his native Southey, Saskatchewan at the age of twelve. Coming to the University of British Columbia in 1944, he curled, played baseball and football, and held the light-heavyweight boxing championship for two years. He played for the Vancouver Blue

Bombers in 1946 when they won the B.C. junior football crown.[29] Residing in Kimberley from 1950-58, Moscovitz played second on the Harold Jordan British Columbia Curling Championship rink of 1956.[30]

210. SAUL LECHTZIER (third from left), Inducted into British Columbia Bowling Hall of Fame, Vancouver, B.C., January 1976.

Mr. Lechtzier was named to the Bowling Section of the B.C. Sports Hall of Fame for his important contributions to the sport over a period of forty years.[31]

In October 1927 the Lechtzier brothers Samuel, Saul, and Harris opened La Salle Recreations at 945 Granville Street, Vancouver. This was the first "modern" bowling centre on the entire Pacific Coast, modelled after the leading bowling establishments of the day in Chicago. In 1941 Saul gave the sport another "shot in the arm," opening the De Luxe Bowling Centre with twenty alleys at 420 Homer Street.[32] The Lechtziers were instrumental in organizing many five-pin and ten-pin leagues in the city. During World War II, Saul organized the Burrard Shipyard League, the world's largest bowling league at that time. He introduced women's bowling into Western Canada.

Saul Lechtzier organized the Bowling Proprietors' Association of British Columbia in 1942, and later the Bowling Proprietors' Association of Canada, being elected first president of both.[33] These organizations stimulated the growth of bowling into a multi-million dollar industry in Canada. In 1959 he submitted a brief to the Chant Royal Commission, advocating a bowling program for B.C. schools, which was adopted.[34] He was also instrumental in having bowling introduced at the University of British Columbia as an accredited sport.

BOWLING CUP, Vancouver Hebrew Athletic Club,
Won by A. M. Silverson, 1929-30.

# 24

## THE ARTS

The Jewish people brought with them to British Columbia a long tradition in the cultural field. In Victoria they participated in the organization and production of music and drama. The Belascos became the most famous of the early Victoria Jewish families. The Franklin brothers were also talented. Selim was active in the Amateur Dramatic Association. Both Selim and Lumley were among the founders and on the Executive Committee of the Victoria Philharmonic Society.[1] Lumley reportedly sang *Di Piscatore* from Lucretia Borgia, and Selim rendered a solo *Over the Green Sea* at its concert in May 1859.[2] Emil Sutro was on the Board of Directors of the Phillharmonic Society in 1861.[3] Victoria-born Samuel Schultz was a talented musician and composed the military march *Charge at Dawn* in honour of the men who fell at Paardeburg in the South African War.[4]

Marcus R. Mayer, of the pioneer Nanaimo family, started off as an apprentice in the *Colonist* composing room. By 1867 he had started a stage career in San Francisco. In his astrakhan-trimmed coat, striped trousers, white gaiters over patent-leather shoes, bejeweled tiepin, and silver-headed cane he gained international fame as playwrite and mentor to such stage greats as Edwin Booth and Sarah Bernhardt.[5]

Later, when Vancouver became the cultural centre of the province, the Jewish people continued to participate in the performing arts, and were in the forefront as sponsors and patrons.

### 211. HUMPHREY, REINA, AND DAVID BELASCO, Theatre Family of Victoria, B.C.

The formative years of David Belasco,[6] one of the greatest names in American theatre, were spent in Victoria. His father Humphrey Abraham Belasco was an aspiring actor in San Francisco. When David was five the family moved north, arriving in Victoria by sail boat in 1858. The elder Belasco joined the local Royal Theatre Company, but was not successful. So he left the family in the capital while he went off to the Cariboo gold fields. There he engaged in tobacco trade with the Indians and trappers, and also took part in prospecting and mining. Meanwhile Mrs. Belasco, who legend has it was the first woman to cross the Isthmus of Panama, opened a store on Johnson Street.

David Belasco attended school in Victoria with "white boys and black boys, Hebrews and Gentiles, rich and poor."[7] He read a good deal, which pleased his father who wanted him to become a rabbi. But his first love was for the theatre. As a little boy he would collect bottles and sell them to buy tickets to the local theatre. He remembered being carried on the stage of the Victoria Theatre in 1858 as "Caro's child" in *Pizarro*. When Julia Dean played in Victoria David had a small part, and in 1864 at the age of eleven, he played the "Duke of York" with Charles Kean in *Richard III*. Soon after, young Belasco ran off to join a travelling circus where he fell ill from a fever and nearly died.

A prolific playwrite, director, skilled scenic designer, and lighting artist, in 1907 he built the Stuyvesant (later Belasco) Theatre in New York. At the time of his death in 1931, David Belasco was one of the leading theatre men in America.

212. MAHRER'S OPERA HOUSE (centre), Nanaimo, B.C.

John Mahrer became a leading public-spirited citizen of Nanaimo. He built the Opera House in 1890, a substantial brick building for a city of five thousand persons, "as a strictly first-class theatre, at popular prices . . . with our own stock company, composed of the best Eastern people."[8] In the fall of 1890 a "Grand Opening Ball" was held in the adjoining Windsor House (left). Demolished in 1941, the site became part of a modern hotel complex whose main ballroom is still known as "The Opera House."[9]

213. SIMON LEISER, Patron of the Arts, Victoria, B.C.

Leiser was actively identified with the Victoria Opera House Company. He took a leading part in building of the Royal Victoria Theatre, making the inaugural address when the building was opened in December 1913. On that occasion he was presented with a loving cup. Later a bust was placed in the lobby of the theatre in memory of his services.[10]

214. "MARY LIVINGSTONE," Radio Star. Photo Vancouver, B.C., ca. 1920.

*L to R:* Sadie Marks, Babe Marks, Leah Wagner.

David Marks was a familiar sight operating a steam suit-pressing machine in the window of his tailor shop on Richards Street. He was president of Schara Tzedeck from 1917-21 at the time the congregation was incorporated, and during the building period of the synagogue.[11]

Many visiting performers found their way to the Marks' home to see Babe the popular elder daughter. Benny Kubelsky of Waukegan, Illinois was playing the Orpheum circuit along with the Marx brothers in 1922. Benny accompanied Zeppo Marx to a family Passover *seder* at the Marks', and was attracted to younger thirteen-year-old daughter Sadie. The couple married in 1927. In the heyday of radio, under the stage names of Jack Benny and Mary Livingstone, they became the world-renowned and loved comedy team.

Through forty-eight years of marriage, the Bennys returned to Vancouver, on occasion, to give benefit performances.[12] In April 1974, a few months before his death at age eighty,[13] Jack Benny was in town to perform in aid of the "save the Orpheum" campaign, the same theatre that he had played in the 1920s.[14]

215. HARRY WOOLFE, Movie Man. Photo at RNWMP Riding School, Regina, Saskatchewan, 1916.

Harry Woolfe was in the motion picture business for fifty years. Originally from Calgary, his career started out with the Royal North West Mounted Police in Saskatchewan, where he became the force's youngest constable at age seventeen, going overseas when the "Mounties" went as a unit with Lord Strathcona Horse in World War I.[15]

After completing his service, Woolfe went to Cincinatti, Ohio for Universal Pictures, riding horseback through the hills of Kentucky with his contracts in a saddle bag, and a pistol in his holster in case he ran into "moonshiners" or obstreperous "hillbillies."

Head of distribution in British Columbia for United Artists, the movie-making corporation established by Charles Chaplin, Mary Pickford, and Douglas Fairbanks, Harry Woolfe retired in 1969 after twenty-six years with the company.[16]

216. KING EDWARD HIGH SCHOOL ORCHESTRA, 1922.

Had two members of the Jewish community: Eugene Mahrer (top right), and Norman Brown (top third from right).

217. LEONARD FRANK, Master Photographer. Photo above Lake O'Hara, Rocky Mountains, 20 July 1924.

A Jew from Oldenburg, Germany, born in 1871, Frank came to the Pacific Coast at the age of twenty-one, travelling in steerage to San Francisco to find his fortune in gold. In 1894, through his contact with miners, he was drawn to Victoria, pushing on to Alberni, which became his territory. There he got into copper mining, opened a general store where, after obtaining citizenship, he became Postmaster in 1903.

Leonard Frank never discovered gold. Instead he left British Columbia a priceless legacy. By chance he won a raffle prize of a crude camera at the Alberni mining camp. This started his brilliant career. His photographs in Alberni include the last stagecoach leaving, the first train arriving, and the first lumber cars to leave Vancouver Island's West Coast.

Determined that photography would be his life's goal, Frank came to Vancouver in 1916, opening a shop and laboratory at 553 Granville Street. Known as an "all-round" photographer, his fame spread quickly. He took photographs for the Vancouver *Daily Province*, and had his work published in magazines such as *National Geographic* and the *Saturday*

*Evening Post.* He was official photographer for the Vancouver Board of Trade, and carried out assignments for the provincial and federal governments. His view of Burrard Inlet was featured on the Canadian 1938 fifty cents postage stamp. Frank's British Columbia pictorial exhibit was admired by thousands at the San Francisco International Exposition. His camera also captured thousands of famous people.

But Frank's chief love was nature and the outdoors. This diminutive five-feet tall photographer, described as "tough as a piece of wire rope when it came to trekking in logging country," endured many hardships of climate and terrain to achieve the ultimate in photographic results. For his field work in 1923, he was honored with the Trail Rider and Mountaineer Badge presented by the CPR representative. In 1938 Frank became an Associate of the Royal Photographic Society of Great Britain, the first in Vancouver to achieve this distinction.

On 24 February 1944 Leonard Frank, a bachelor, died in his sleep aged seventy-three, having spent fifty years photographing British Columbia. He left behind one of the most valuable historic treasures of British Columbia's recorded history. More than a third of the 100,000 photographs in the B.C. Historic Photograph Section of Vancouver Public Library were his. His collection is regarded by experts as the most important in the West and the second most significant in all of Canada. His collection in the field of logging is probably the best in the world.[17]

218. VIEW OF BURRARD INLET, VANCOUVER HARBOR, Canada Postage Stamp, Issued June 1938. Based on Photo by Leonard Frank.

219. ALFRED A. EVANS, Actor, Vancouver, B.C. Photo 1931.

Alfred Evans was prominent in theatrical productions in Vancouver for twenty-five years as actor, playwrite, director, and executive.

For four years Evans played leading roles with the Players' Club of the University of British Columbia, such as the younger son in Noel Coward's *The Young Idea*. On graduation in 1931, he was offered a scholarship at Harvard's Baker School of Playwriting, but chose a business career instead.

In 1933 Alfred Evans joined the Vancouver Little Theatre Association, and was involved in leading roles in most of their plays through the 1930s and 40s including: *Judgment Day*, *Idiot's Delight*, *Night Must Fall*, and *Guest in the House*. In 1947 he became vice-president and subsequently president of the Association.[18]

220. A JEWISH PRODIGY, At Age Ten, Vancouver, B.C., May 1933.

Ten-year-old Nathan Rothstein, a brilliant young violinist of the Vancouver Jewish community, was awarded the Women's Canadian Club Scholarship in competition with students up to nineteen years of age.[19]

Leaving Vancouver to continue his musical studies, he was a violinist with the San Francisco Symphony and later with Henry King's Orchestra.[20]

221. RALPH FROMSON, In Gilbert and Sullivan Opera, Victoria, B.C., 1938.

"Possessing a fine baritone singing voice," Fromson performed in numerous light opera productions. He was a member of Beth Israel Choir, and took a leading part in the B'nai B'rith Singing Degree Team.[21]

Son of Eli Fromson, a career soldier of the Royal Canadian Ordinance Corps, Esquimalt, Ralph also served the entire World War II as a warrant officer in the RCOC.

His wife Anna (Goldberg) was the first secretary of the Jewish Community Centre and of the Vancouver Jewish Administrative Council.[22]

222. THE DIRECTORS, Hosts of Kitsilano Show Boat, Vancouver, B.C. Photo 1954.

Mr. and Mrs. I. Director were pioneers in the formative years of Prince Rupert and Prince George. Mrs. Director was prominent in musical circles in these northern cities. She was a violinist in the thirty-five piece Prince Rupert Symphony Orchestra. She also took part there in amateur dramatics. On one occasion, an itinerant Catholic priest wished to hold midnight mass in South Fort George, and finding no Catholics with the necessary musical ability, called upon Mrs. Director and other musicians, none of whom were Catholic.[23]

The Directors came to Vancouver in 1922. For over thirty years they were official hosts of the Kitsilano Show Boat, a unique waterfront stage, which provided a training ground for young talent, and summer entertainment for local residents.[24] She was also a president of Kitsilano Choir, and sang with their two daughters in the Brahms Choir.

In long and fruitful lifetimes, through sixty-four years of marriage, Isidor and Hannah Director exemplified the pioneer spirit in British Columbia.[25] In 1961 they were awarded, as a team, the Don Brown Trophy as "outstanding citizens."[26]

223. GEORGE B. ZUKERMAN, Internationally-Acclaimed Solo Bassoonist.[27]

English-born George Zukerman came to the United States during World War II, where his father was a correspondent for several New York Yiddish newspapers. He first played with the Vancouver Symphony Orchestra in 1950 on invitation from New York. While here he met and married Netta Karmel, a social worker with the Jewish Family Welfare Bureau. In 1951 Zukerman was invited by Leonard Bernstein to become a member of the Israel Philharmonic Orchestra.[28]

Taking up permanent residence in Vancouver, in 1953 impresario Zukerman started the Overture Concert Series, touring Canada from the East Coast to the West Coast of Vancouver Island, and pioneering music concerts in the far north where they travelled by dog sled to Tuktoyaktuk on the Arctic Ocean. He also toured the CBC Chamber Orchestra on the *Northland Prince*, playing in villages upcoast as far as the Alaska Border. He has served on the Board of Canada Council.

George Zukerman is the world's only internationally-acclaimed solo bassoonist, and has given recitals in such varied places as Russia and the South Seas.[29]

224. JEWISH COMMUNITY CENTRE ORCHESTRA, Vancouver, B.C. Organized 1963.

When the activities for the new Jewish Community Centre were being formulated, a music program was a prime consideration.[30] Plans were formulated for an orchestra, choir, musical appreciation, and workshops for interested amateurs. A chamber music quartet was initially organized, and performed at the centre in 1963.

Under the leadership of Lionel Goodman, a full string orchestra was formed. Sunday, 19 April 1964 was an auspicious day for the Jewish community of Vancouver, when the orchestra first performed in public at a spring concert. Jerome Glass, Professor of Music at Western Washington State College, was the conductor.[31] "Coming of age" of the orchestra was marked on 24 April 1966 when renowned pianist Jan Cherniavsky[32] was the guest artist at the orchestra's sixth concert, augmented for the occasion by a wind section headed by bassoonist George Zukerman, from the Vancouver Symphony Orchestra.[33]

225. JEWISH COMMUNITY CENTRE CHOIR, In Action During Fifth Anniversary Year, Vancouver, B.C., 1969.[34]

*Back L to R:* Arnold Selwyn, Maurice Moses, Ben Akselrod, Max Rosenthal, Eugene Grabowski, Michael Dymant, Fred Toft, David Rabinovitch, William Ornstein.

*Middle L to R:* Betty Hershberg, Minnie Poskar, Fan Gold, Celia Schachter, Annette Kaplan, Helen Grunfeld, Molly Bekesinski, Ann Rosenthal, Sylvia Avery.

*Front L to R:* Anita Hicks, Susan Hershberg, Lil Lepkin, Marjorie Goldhar, Gertrude Shaffer, Ida Weiner, Bella Bevan, Riessa Carr, Rosette Yehia, Georgina Detwiller.

Conductor is Elizabeth Wolak, and piano accompanist Muriel Morris.

*Missing:* Terry Haughian, Irene Gray, Ada Sorin, Myrna Rothman, Shelley Criddle.

A Vancouver Jewish choir made its public debut in May 1947 at the first Dominion-wide Folk Festival, which took place at the Forum.[35] Synagogue choirs have also performed for the public at large, as well as for traditional religious services.

In October 1964 a Jewish Community Centre choir of thirty members was organized. Six months later in May 1965, at the Kiwanis B.C. Music Festival held in the ballroom of Hotel Vancouver, the choir "presented Hebrew and Yiddish songs to a warm and receptive audience," and placed first. When presenting the trophy, adjudicator Robert Irwin remarked: "The undeniable warmth of your performance came over to me. I regret I didn't understand the language."[36]

During its performances, the choir has traced the history of Jewish music from the beginning to modern times, presenting a repertoire of traditional Yiddish folk songs and Israeli melodies.[37]

# 25

## THE SUMMING UP

Among the prolific histories of British Columbia, the role of the ethnic groups has gone largely unnoticed until recent times. In these pages we have told the story of the Jewish people who have lived in this province for 119 years. Always small in numbers, the Jewish population has grown from the hundred inhabitants of Victoria in 1858 to twelve thousand in the present decade.[1] This is only one-half of one per cent of the total population of B.C. These small numbers belie the vibrant, even vital element that Jews have contributed, particularly in the pioneering era of the province. Among their numbers have been included not only gold miners, packers, pedlars, traders, merchants but also ministers of government, justices of the courts, professors and chancellors of universities, doctors, sportsmen, men and women of the arts, leaders in social and community services. What is the state of the Jewish communities today?

There are few frontiers remaining in British Columbia. The post-World War II industrialization of the province, with centralization of the majority of the population in the major cities, has resulted in the dissolution of the small-town Jewish communities. Today, no organized Jewish community life exists in the province nor in the Yukon, outside of Metropolitan Vancouver and Victoria.

In the post-war decades, the Jewish population of British Columbia has been augmented by new immigrations from Europe, the Near East, Far East, and South America, resulting in a more varied and cosmopolitan community. But more significantly, the bulk of the increase has been Canadian-born, coming from the Prairie Provinces and Central Canada after servicemen "discovered" B.C. during the war. The gold miner and pedlar have disappeared. Only a few of the old-style Jewish merchants persist in the old part of town. Occupations have become much more diversified, involving participation in virtually all fields.

The Jewish communities of British Columbia, with ninety-five percent of the population now resident within the Greater Vancouver Regional District, continue to be in a healthy state. Jewish organizations, schools,[2] community centre, youth groups, senior citizens facilities, social services, and performing groups still are a positive, creative force in the province. While the communities face the common problem of the rebellion of many modern youths to tradition values, Jewish education has been upgraded with the formation of a Jewish High School, and introduction of Judaic

Studies courses in the university curriculum. Adult Jewish studies and Hebrew night school courses are given. Creation of the modern State of Israel has resulted in a spiritual and cultural renaissance for the Jewish people as a whole. While many Jews have visited, helped with financial support, and youths have studied and worked in *kibbutzim* there, relatively few British Columbians have emigrated to Israel. Most chose to keep Canada as their home, where they live in conditions of relative affluence, security, freedom, and fulfillment, perhaps not exceeded anywhere else in the world.

A high proportion of Jews continue to attend religious services, some if only for the High Holy Days. While Orthodoxy still flourishes, preserving the ancient faith, rituals, and customs, it now represents a minority in the community. The middle-of-the-road Conservative congregations have attracted the majority of synagogue-goers in British Columbia. Their services attempt to reconcile the traditional values of Judaism with modern forms, such as more English-speaking content, and moves towards equality for women. Totally Reform practices have not caught on here to the extent that they have in the United States.

There has never been a significant, overt manifestation of anti-Semitism in British Columbia. This may be owing to such factors as the small number of Jews, the demand for their skills in a pioneering society, and their adaptability to the majority culture. The Jewish population, being white and often unnoticed, and having a background in Western society, did not suffer the deplorable discrimination of the kind experienced by Orientals and East Asiatics. Nevertheless there has been latent discrimination in such areas as employment and private clubs. With their long history in the province, and their greater acceptance in the established society, there is less tendency now to regard the Jewish people as an alien group.[3]

Like most minorities in Canada, the Jewish communities continue to resist the pressures and conveniences of melding into a completely homogeneous society, while at the same time recognizing that a Canadian identity has emerged. Since the "walls of the *ghetto*" have crumbled, there has followed mixing and intermarriage of the younger generations with the overall population on a scale undreamed of by their grandparents. And the population ranges from those who are completely assimilated into the predominant culture, to Jews who hold no formal community affiliation, to those who maintain an active role in Jewish community affairs. Canadians and British Columbians have not accepted the melting-pot ideology on the American model, whereby the ethnic elements are expected to submerge their particular diversities into a predominant North-American culture. Rather, Canadians have actively fostered a multi-ethnic society made up of a mosaic of individual cultures bonded together for the commonweal.[4] Within this framework the Jewish minority will take its part in the future development of the province, as an identifiable group maintaining the institutions and values of Judaism, under conditions of freedom and equality enjoyed by all Canadians.

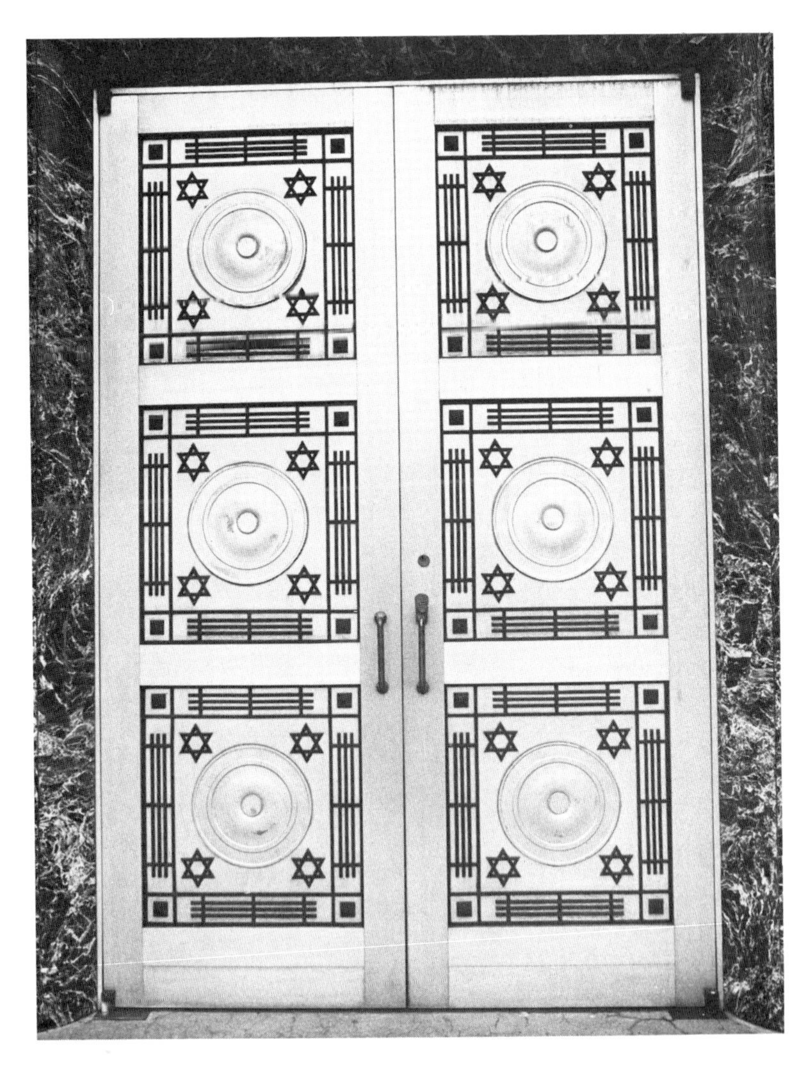

DOOR, Second Schara Tzedeck Synagogue, Vancouver, B.C.

# PHOTOGRAPH CREDITS

Frontispiece: Ben Pastinsky

1. Provincial Archives of British Columbia (PABC)
2. PABC
3. PABC
4. Jewish Historical Society of British Columbia Archives (JHSBC)
5. PABC
6. C. E. Leonoff photo
7. PABC
8. PABC
9. Sonia Rose
10. Leonoff photo
11. Sonia Rose
12. JHSBC
13. PABC
14. Photos by Gibson; Julius B. Jaffe
15. Julius B. Jaffe
16. Benjamin Grossman
17. PABC
18. PABC
19. PABC
20. Mrs. J. (Sonia) Rose
21. Ron Greene
22. JHSBC
23. Josephine Lancaster
24. Irving Strickland photo; *Victoria Times*
25. Leonoff photo
26. McAlpin & Lamb, photographers, Portland, Oregon; PABC
27. PABC
28. John Cass
29. Helen Olfman
30. PABC
31. Bureau of Mines, PABC
32. PABC
33. Isidor Director
34. Isidor Director
35. Esmond Lando
36. Horace Ripstein
37. PABC
38. PABC
39. Frances Panar
40. Williams Bros. photo; Samuel Heller
41. Leonoff photo
42. Leonoff photo
43. George Biely
44. Samuel Sussel
45. Mrs. N. J. (Sally) Tall; and Leonoff photo
46. Leonoff photo
47. PABC

48. PABC
49. L. A. Blanc Photographic Gallery, Barkerville, B.C.; PABC
50. PABC
51. Linda (Spaner) Dayan
52. PABC
53. Adella (Woogman) Moscovitz
54. Leopold Levey
55. Mrs. J. (Olive) Segal
56. Mrs. S. (Bessy) Wise
57. Clara (Wise) Waldman
58. Margaret Tooley
59. Sonia (Robinson) Rose
60. Sonia (Robinson) Rose
61. Mrs. M. B. (Rose) Cohen
62. Jacob Leith
63. Mrs. J. (Ann) Spaner
64. Rosalie (Director) Gorosh
65. Canadian Jewish Congress (CJC)
66. Mrs. C. (Lily) Graham
67. Graphic photo: *Jewish Western Bulletin* (*Bulletin*)
68. Arthur Zimmerman
69. Arthur Zimmerman
70. Walter Mackay Draycott
71. Dr. Irving Snider photo
72. Harold Koffman
73. Theresa (Blumberg) Kaufmann
74. Mrs. W. (Ray) Morris
75. Dr. Maurice Fox
76. Dr. Leon Komar
77. Dr. Irving Snider
78. Dr. Irving Ziskrout
79. Mrs. J. I. (Rosalie) Gorosh
80. Michael Ratner
81. Leonoff photo
82. Harry Weinstein
83. Ann (Goldberg) (Fromson) Muskovitch
84. PABC
85. JHSBC
86. JHSBC
87. Horace Ripstein
88. JHSBC
89. The Vandeysant Galleries; Budd Sugarman
90. Krass Studio; *Bulletin*
91. Irma Zack
92. Bernard Reed
93. Julius B. Jaffe
94. Louis Checov
95. *Bulletin*

96. JHSBC
97. Frema Marshall
98. JHSBC
99. Morris Saltzman; CJC
100. JHSBC
101. Hannah Director
102. Sam Shine
103. Leonard Frank photo; Vancouver Public Library (VPL)
104. JHSBC
105. Dorothy Grossman
106. Morris Saltzman; CJC
107. Al Commercial Photo Service; Ben Pastinsky
108. Steffens-Colmer photo: I. S. Finkelman
109. JHSBC
110. *Bulletin*
111. Josepho Studios; Barbara (Taylor) Freedman
112. *Bulletin*
113. Graphic Industries photo; JHSBC
114. Franz Lindner photo; Pioneer Women
115. Vancouver City Archives
116. Eudelle (Veno) Wall
117. JHSBC
118. JHSBC
119. Morris Saltzman
120. Leonard Frank photo; Alfred Evans
121. Mitchell Snider
122. Sam Flader
123. Rose (Goldberg) Youngson
124. Eudelle (Veno) Wall
125. Myer Freedman
126. Philip Timms photo; VPL
127. Leonoff photo
128. Philip Timms photo; VPL
129. Leonard Frank photo; Myer Felstein; and Leonoff photo
130. Leonard Frank photo; VPL
131. Vancouver City Archives
132. Leonoff photo
133. JHSBC
134. Mrs. M. Wine
135. Violet (Weinrobe) Franklin
136. Marlowe photo; Myer Felstein
137. Leonard Frank photo; VPL
138. Myer Felstein
139. Al's Photo Service; Julius Stusser
140. JHSBC
141. Mrs. W. (Ray) Morris
142. Leonoff photo
143. Deni Eagland photo; *Vancouver Sun*

144. Leonoff photo
145. Mitchell Snider
146. JHSBC
147. JHSBC
148. JHSBC
149. JHSBC
150. JHSBC
151. *Bulletin*
152. Dr. Irving Snider
153. JHSBC
154. Joseph Youngson
155. JHSBC
156. Anne Wyne
157. Mrs. J. I. (Rosalie) Gorosh
158. *Bulletin*
159. JHSBC
160. JHSBC
161. *Bulletin*
162. Harry Toban
163. Alvin Narod
164. Reuben H. Marlow Studio; Maury Rothstein
165. Morry Harrison
166. Mort Raels
167. Clara (Wise) Waldman
168. E. M. Allen Photo Centre; JHSBC
169. National Council of Jewish Women
170. Franz Lindner photo; *Bulletin*
171. Dave Zeffert
172. PABC
173. PABC
174. William Notman photo, Ottawa; PABC
175. Frederic's Foto Studio, Prince George, B.C.; Mrs. C. (Lily) Graham
176. Leonoff photo
177. Schiffer Photography; City of New Westminster
178. *Bulletin*
179. Benjamin Grossman
180. Philip Waterman
181. *Bulletin*
182. Mollie (Mickelson) Klein
183. Al's Photo Service; *Bulletin*
184. *Bulletin*
185. *Bulletin*
186. Leopold Levey
187. JHSBC
188. David Brown
189. Eudelle (Veno) Wall
190. Frema (Parker) Marshall
191. Joseph Morris

192. Julius B. Jaffe
193. W. J. Moore photo; Mrs. M. (Rose) Soskin
194. Julius Stusser
195. JHSBC
196. *Bulletin*
197. *Bulletin*
198. Dr. Jacob H. Narod
199. Ben Pastinsky
200. Max Poplack
201. Mrs. P. (Rachel) Brotman
202. Alter Silverson
203. Richmond Country Club
204. Morris Saltzman; CJC
205. Al's Photo Service; *Bulletin*
206. *Bulletin*
207. Brian Kent photo; *Bulletin*
208. Gordon Sedawie photo; Vancouver *Province*
209. Les McAuley photo, Moncton, N.B.; William Moscovitz
210. Saul Lechtzier
211. PABC
212. John Cass
213. From a painting in PABC
214. Mission Studio, Vancouver, B.C.; Eudelle (Veno) Wall
215. Harry Woolfe
216. Norman Brown
217. Leonard Frank Photos; *Bulletin*
218. JHSBC
219. *Bulletin*
220. *Bulletin*
221. Mrs. M. (Fromson) Muskovitch
222. Mrs. I. (Hannah) Director
223. *Bulletin*
224. JHSBC
225. *Bulletin*

Other photos by C. E. Leonoff; bowling cup by Commercial Illustrators

# NOTES

## PREFACE

[1] David Rome, *The First Two Years: A Record of the Jewish Pioneers on Canada's Pacific Coast, 1858-1860* (Montreal: H. M. Caiserman, 1942). Hereafter cited as *First Two Years.*

[2] David Rome, "Jewish Pioneers of British Columbia," based on materials in the Bronfman Collection of Jewish Canadiana at the Jewish Public Library of Montreal, Vancouver *Jewish Western Bulletin,* B.C. Centenary Series 1858-1958, 16 August 1957, p. 3. See below for other articles in this series.

[3] Victoria Congregation Emanu-El, "Minute Books," 1862-66, 1886-1900, 1900-22, 1922-31, Provincial Archives of British Columbia (hereafter cited as PABC). Available on microfilm.

[4] *Weekly News: Official Organ of the Vancouver Jewish Community Centre*, vol. 1, no. 1 (21 February 1930) to vol. 1, no. 6 (10 April 1930); Vancouver *Jewish Centre News*, vol. 1, no. 7 (17 April 1930) to vol. 1, no. 30 (2 October 1930); and Vancouver *Jewish Western Bulletin*, vol. 1, no. 31 (9 October 1930) to vol. 44, no. 34 (New Year ed., 8 September 1977). Hereafter cited as *Bulletin.*

[5] Abraham J. Arnold, ed., *Jewish Western Bulletin: B.C. Centenary Edition, 1858-1958*, vol. 26, no. 26 (30 June 1958). Hereafter cited as *Centenary Ed.*

[6] "Jewish Historical Society of B.C. Holds First Meeting," 26 November 1970, *Bulletin,* 4 December 1970, p. 16. "The Jewish Historical Society of British Columbia" was incorporated under Province of British Columbia "Societies Act," 25 January 1971.

[7] "Historical Society to Compile Pictorial Story of B.C. Jewry," Ibid, 25 February 1972, p. 15.

## I IN THE BEGINNING

[1] Bruce A. McKelvie, *Pageant of B.C.* (Toronto: Thomas Nelson & Sons, 1955; 2d B.C. Centennial ed., 1957), pp. 3-4.

[2] Arthur A. Chiel, "So Who Really Discovered America?: A Startling Proposition that Chinese Jews Came to B.C. 700 Years Ago," *Bulletin,* 1 April 1966, p. 49.

[3] "First Jew in the Pacific Northwest?" *Centenary Ed.*, pp. 6, 8; and original MS, n.d. (Handwritten) in possession of Julius Stusser, Vancouver. Copy JHSBC.

## 2 VICTORIA: BIRTHPLACE OF THE COMMUNITIES, 1858

[1] Alfred Waddington, *The Fraser Mines Vindicated* (Victoria: P. De Garro, 1858; Vancouver: Robert R. Reid private press reprint, 1949), p. 30.

[2] Arthur Daniel Hart, comp. and ed., *The Jew in Canada: A Complete Record of Canadian Jewry From the Days of the French Regime to the Present Time* (Toronto and Montreal: Jewish Publications Limited, 1926), p. 57. Hereafter cited as *Jew in Canada.*

[3] *First Two Years*, p. 30.

[4] See Robert E. Levinson, "American Jews in the West," *Western Historical Quarterly*, reprint, vol. 5, no. 3 (July 1974): 285-94. An apropos monograph on merchandising by Jews in the West.

[5] *Jew in Canada*, p. 57.

[6] Norton B. Stern, ed., "A Western Canadian Report of 1859," *Western States Jewish Historical Quarterly*, vol. 9, no. 1 (October 1976): 63-65, quoting San Francisco *Weekly Gleaner*, 4 November 1859, p. 2.
[7] *First Two Years*, pp. 30-31.
[8] See E. W. Wright, ed., *Lewis & Dryden's Marine History of the Pacific Northwest* (Portland: Lewis & Dryden Printing Co., 1895), pp. 69, 223-27 for a history of the *Pacific*, which went down off Cape Flattery in November 1875 with ca. 250 people aboard, regarded as the greatest marine disaster of the time on the Pacific Coast.
[9] *Centenary Ed.*, inside front cover.
[10] Ibid., p. 3.
[11] Ibid.
[12] See *Jew in Canada*, p. 118, for a biography of Sylvester.
[13] *First Two Years*, pp. 6-7.
[14] See *Jew in Canada*, p. 561, for a biography of Davies.
[15] "Pioneer Synagogue Builder," *Centenary Ed.*, p. 57.
[16] Elizabeth Lamont Forbes, "A Jewish Home," *Wild Roses at Their Feet: Pioneer Women of Vancouver Island* (Vancouver: British Columbia Centennial '71 Committee, 1971), pp. 32-33.
[17] *Jew in Canada*, p. 240.
[18] Naomi Pellin, "Women's Role in History of B.C. Jewish Community," *Centenary Ed.*, p. 19.
[19] *First Two Years*, p. 8.
[20] Victoria *British Colonist*, 18 May 1859, p. 3; and 20 May 1859, p. 3.
[21] *First Two Years*, pp. 31-32.
[22] *British Colonist*, 25 May 1859, p. 2; and 6 June 1859, p. 2.
[23] *First Two Years*, p. 33.
[24] Rome, "Jewish Pioneers," and *History of Grand Lodge of British Columbia 1871-1970* (Victoria: Grand Lodge of British Columbia AF&AM, 1971), pp. 393-95.
[25] *First Two Years*, p. 31.
[26] Stern, p. 65.
[27] *First Two Years*, p. 34.
[28] Ibid., pp. 17-18; and David Rome, "Lewis Lewis: Pioneer Synagogue Builder," *Bulletin*, Centenary Series, 18 October 1957, p. 6.
[29] *Grand Lodge*, pp. 37, 39; and David Rome, "Legend of the Victoria Synagogue," *Bulletin*, 16 May 1935, p. 1.
[30] Inscription on gravestone.
[31] *British Colonist*, 17 November 1866; and David Rome, "Herman Schultz Father of Judge Schultz," *Bulletin*, Centenary Series, 23 January 1959, p. 7.
[32] Published sources on Temple Emanu-El of Victoria are numerous. The following have been referred to: "Congregation Emanu-El, Victoria, B.C.," *Jew in Canada*, p. 117; Rev. Dr. J. K. Unsworth, "Jews of Victoria Dedicated Temple Emanu-El in 1863," Victoria *Daily Colonist*, 7 February 1932, reprinted in *Centenary Ed.*, p. 7; Vivienne Chadwick, "The Pioneers' Synagogue: From a Dry Goods Shop to Temple Emanuel," *Bulletin*, 19 September 1963, pp. 17-20, reprinted from *Daily Colonist*; and Allan Klenman, comp. for Jewish Historical Society of British Columbia, "Victoria Was First B.C. Jewish Centre," *Bulletin*, British Columbia Centennial '71, 8 April 1971, pp. 49-56.
[33] *First Two Years*, p. 30; and David Rome, "Rosh Hashona 5719; Centennial of First Jewish New Year Services Over a Quarter of the Globe," *Bulletin*, 12 September 1958, pp. 5, 38, quoting *Victoria Gazette*, 24 August 1858, Notice: "A meeting will be held on Sunday next, August 29, . . . at Mr. Gambitz's store on Government St., . . . for the purpose of securing a place of meeting for the ensuing Holidays . . ." The meeting, chaired by Charles Davis, was reported in *Weekly Gleaner*, 8 September 1858, p. 5.
[34] "Trials and Tribulations of Victoria Synagogue Builders in 1863," *Bulletin*, 25 September 1957, pp. 4, 6, 80, 82.

[35] The original handwritten subscription list is on display in the synagogue. A typewritten copy prepared by Allan Klenman is in Jewish Historical Society of British Columbia Archives (hereafter cited as JHSBC).

[36] *British Colonist*, 3 June 1863, p. 3.

[37] Ibid.

[38] Daisy Minchin and Josephine Lancaster, taped interview by C. E. Leonoff, Victoria, 23 July 1972. JHSBC.

[39] Office of the Chief Rabbi, London to the President of the Hebrew Congregation, Victoria, 11 February 5623 (1863), Congregation Emanu-El, "Minutes of Regular Quarterly Meeting," 29 June 1863; See also "Pastoral From the Chief Rabbi and the Congregation's Reply," *Bulletin*, 25 September 1957, p. 6.

[40] *Centenary Ed.*, pp. 48-49, 53; and Mrs. Joseph (Sonia) Rose, taped interview by C. E. Leonoff, Victoria, 27 March 1972. JHSBC.

[41] See *Jew in Canada*, p. 146, for a biography of Berner; and Louis Rosenberg, "Rabbi Marcus Berner of Hirsch and Victoria," *Centenary Ed.*, p. 12, reprinted from Winnipeg *Israelite Press*, 24 June 1941, p. 1.

[42] Cited from description of photo in PABC.

[43] Arthur Levy, Deep Cove, B.C. to Ed. Mallek, Victoria, n.d. (Handwritten). Contains brief biographies of many of the early Jews in Victoria including members of the Levy family. JHSBC.

[44] Vancouver Jewish Community *Centre Bulletin*, 9 February 1929, p. 1; Edgar Fawcett, *Some Reminiscences of Old Victoria* (Toronto: William Briggs, 1912), pp. 92-99, gives a history of the "Fires and Firemen" of early Victoria including a section by H. F. Levy on "The Pioneer Engines," pp. 97-99.

[45] A. J. Arnold, "B'nai B'rith Family in British Columbia Is 48 Years Old," *Centenary Ed.*, p. 30.

[46] *Jew in Canada*, p. 436.

[47] Arthur Levy.

[48] George Inglis, "B.C.'s Earliest Motor Car Man," *Daily Colonist*, 6 December 1970, pp. 6-7.

[49] Benjamin Grossman, taped interview by C. E. Leonoff, Victoria, 27 March 1972. JHSBC.

[50] *First Two Years*, p. 13.

[51] Fewcett, pp. 57-72, gives a "Street History" describing the business premises of downtown Victoria in the 1860s.

[52] D. W. Higgins, *The Mystic Spring: And Other Tales of Western Life* (Toronto: William Briggs, 1904), p. 165.

[53] *First Two Years*, pp. 8-12.

[54] Ibid., pp. 22-23; and David Rome, "The Sutros of Victoria: 1," *Bulletin*, Centenary Series, 19 December 1957, p. 14; and Ibid., "Sutros: 2," 7 February 1958, p. 6.

[55] *Jew in Canada*, pp. 58, 119.

[56] Harry Gregson, *A History of Victoria* (West Vancouver: J. J. Douglas, 1970), p. 199.

[57] See *Bulletin*, 10 March 1949, p. 1 for obituary of Joseph Rose; and Sonia Rose interview.

[58] See *Bulletin*, 21 April 1972, p. 6, for obituary of Morris Greene.

[59] Baron Maurice de Hirsch: German-Jewish financier and philanthropist who dedicated his fortune to the welfare of East European Jews, towards agricultural colonies and trade schools in North and South America.

[60] *Jew in Canada*, p. 116.

[61] *Jewish Centre News*, 29 May 1930, p. 1.

[62] *Bulletin*, 9 May 1935, p. 1; See also Ibid., 20 June 1935, pp. 1-2, obituary; and *Centenary Ed.*, p. 60.

[63] "Harry L. Salmon: Oldest Jew in B.C.," *Bulletin*, 23 March 1956, pp. 10-12; and Minchin (daughter) and Lancaster (niece) interview.

[64] Obituary, *Bulletin*, 2 May 1958, p. 2; and *Centenary Ed.*, p. 60.

[65] *Bulletin*, 1 August 1958, pp. 1-2.
[66] CJVI, Victoria, "Enterprise in Action," 5 March 1961, "The Story of the Mallek Family of Vancouver and Victoria," Hugh Curtis. Taped copy JHSBC.
[67] Pellin, "Women's Role."
[68] Minchin and Lancaster interview.

## 3 NANAIMO

[1] John Cass, "From 'Red House' to 'Red Carpet'," Nanaimo, September 1967. (Typewritten). Copy JHSBC.
[2] John Cass, "Marcus Wolfe," Nanaimo, n.d. (Typewritten). Copy JHSBC.
[3] *British Colonist*, 22 August 1860.
[4] *Grand Lodge*, p. 22.
[5] Klenman, "Victoria First Centre," p. 56.
[6] *Grand Lodge*, p. 23.
[7] Allan Klenman, "Pioneer Jews in Early B.C.: 1858-1875," Victoria, March 1971, p. 10. (Typewritten). Copy JHSBC. This MS contains names and brief biographies of the hundred known Jews of B.C. in this period.
[8] *Grand Lodge*, pp. 116-17.
[9] Ibid., p. 626.
[10] Klenman, "Pioneer Jews," p. 11.
[11] *Grand Lodge*, pp. 159, 531, 635.
[12] J. B. Kerr, *Biographical Dictionary of Well-Known British Columbians* (Vancouver: Kerr & Begg, 1890), pp. 224-25.
[13] "Nanaimo Merchant Called Away," *Nanaimo Free Press*, 3 September 1912, p. 1. Obituary of John Mahrer.
[14] C. W. Parker, ed., *Who's Who and Why: A Biographical Dictionary of Notable Men and Women of Western Canada*, vol. 2 (1912): 522; and Information from Helen Olfman, Vancouver, 1977.

## 4 NORTHWEST COAST

[1] First Two Years, pp. 10-11.
[2] J. Turner-Turner, *Three Years' Hunting and Trapping in America and the Great North-West* (London: Maclure, 1888), pp. 44-45.
[3] Bruce Ramsey, *Britannia: The Story of a Mine* (Britannia Beach: Community Club, 1967), pp. 20-23, 27-28, 39.
[4] Stewart T. McNeill, "The Spirit of Britannia's Past," *Westworld*, September-October 1976, p. 23.
[5] Sources on Moss are: J. B. Kerr, pp. 235-41; Capt. John T. Walbran, *British Columbia Coast Names 1592-1906: Their Origin and History* (Ottawa: Government Printing Bureau, 1909), pp. 343-44; and Jan Williams, "The Mystery of Morris Moss," *Westworld*, September-October, 1977, pp. 20-22, 34.
[6] Naomi Pellin, "The Directors: An Outstanding Pioneer Couple," *Bulletin*, 2 March 1956, p. 8.
[7] Mrs. M. B. (Rose) Cohen, taped interview by C. E. Leonoff, Vancouver, 30 September 1976. JHSBC.
[8] Mrs. Rosalie (Director) Gorosh, taped interview by C. E. Leonoff, Vancouver, 15 July 1977. JHSBC.
[9] Esmond Lando, taped reminiscences, Vancouver, August 1976. JHSBC.
[10] Esmond Lando, taped interview by C. E. Leonoff, Vancouver, 12 July 1977. JHSBC.
[11] Horace Ripstein (grandson), taped interview by A. M. Freedman, Montreal, 3 February 1975. JHSBC.

## 5 NEW WESTMINSTER AND THE FRASER VALLEY

1. "Conditions in the Cariboo Gold Fields in 1861," quoting from *Papers Relative to B.C.*, Part IV, *Centenary Ed.*, p. 8. Levi was the Cariboo managing partner in Barkerville.
2. *Bulletin*, 8 April 1971, p. 45.
3. *First Two Years*, pp. 21-22; and David Rome, "The Reinhardts: Pioneers of New Westminster," *Bulletin*, Centenary Series, 15 November 1957, p. 8.
4. *First Two Years*, p. 21, quoting *Occident*, 1855, p. 419, from California *Democrat.*
5. Rome, "Reinhardts."
6. *Bulletin*, 30 March 1950, p. 8.
7. For information on Louis and Dina Zack see *Bulletin*: 6 April 1955, p. 2; 10 May 1957, p. 5; 16 December 1960, p. 6; and 5 January 1962, p. 5.
8. Samuel Heller, taped interview by C. E. Leonoff, Vancouver, 1 September 1976. JHSBC.
9. *Bulletin*, 11 March 1966, p. 5; and 17 March 1967, p. 9.
10. Citation in possession of S. Heller.
11. *Vancouver Sun*, 21 December 1966, p. 6; and Jack Wasserman, Ibid., 22 December 1966, p. 25.
12. Harry Toban, taped interview by A. Krieger and I. Dodek, Vancouver, 22 June 1971. JHSBC.
13. Samuel Zack, taped interview by C. E. Leonoff, Vancouver, 20 May 1976. JHSBC.
14. Patrick Durant, "Hotel King," *Province*, 29 June 1977, pp. 13-14.
15. *Bulletin*, 29 May 1975, p. 1.
16. *First Two Years*, pp. 18-19, quoting *British Colonist*, 11, 25 December 1858.
17. "Birthplace of British Columbia," *Beautiful British Columbia*, vol. 18, no. 4 (Spring 1977): 42-46.
18. Information from George Biely, Vancouver.
19. "Royal Society Elects Biely," *Bulletin*, 6 May 1966, p. 5.
20. Samuel and Anne Sussel, taped interview by C. E. Leonoff, Chilliwhack, 24 May 1976. JHSBC.
21. Mrs. N. J. (Sally) Tall, taped interview by A. M. Freedman, Palm Springs, California, 6 November 1976. JHSBC.
22. Werner and Ingrid Bick, taped interview by C. E. Leonoff, Aldergrove, 28 July 1976. JHSBC.

## 6 GOLD: FRASER RIVER — BARKERVILLE

1. David Rome, "First Days of the Oppenheimers in B.C.," *Bulletin*, Centenary Series, 14 March 1958, p. 6; David Rome, "The Oppenheimers of British Columbia," *Canadian Jewish Year Book*, 3 vols. (Montreal: Canadian Jewish Year Book Reg'd., 1939-42), 1 (1939-40), reprinted in *Centenary Ed.*, p. 9; and Jim Nesbitt, "Old Homes and Families," *Daily Colonist*, 5 November 1953, p. 6.
2. A. C. Milliken, Yale, to Phyllis Sapers, Canadian Jewish Congress, Vancouver, 28 February 1977. Copy JHSBC.
3. David Rome, "Jews in the Cariboo," *Year Book*, 1, reprinted in *Centenary Ed.*, p. 6.
4. Rome, "Oppenheimers."
5. David Rome, "Chas. Oppenheimer and the Cariboo Road," *Bulletin*, Centenary Series, 30 May 1958, p. 8.
6. Mrs. Jack (Ann) Spaner and Linda (Spaner) Dayan (daughter), taped interview by C. E. Leonoff, Richmond, B.C., 16 April 1976. JHSBC.

## 7 SOUTHERN INTERIOR

1. Mrs. Clare McAllister, Victoria, daughter of M. R. McQuarrie, Mayor of Nelson at the time, to C. E. Leonoff, Vancouver, 21 May 1977. JHSBC. The name derives from the Silver King Mine on Toad Mountain near Nelson.

[2] Dumas Malone, ed., *Dictionary of American Biography* (New York: Charles Scribner's Sons, 1932), 8: 507-8.
[3] Elsie G. Turnbull, "Early Smelters in the South-Eastern Interior," paper delivered 15 May 1960, Grand Forks, B.C., *Boundary Historical Society Fourth Report*, 1964, pp. 5-6.
[4] "Mr. Heinze's Rising Star," *Daily Colonist*, 11 April 1900, p. 6; See also obituary, Vancouver *News-Advertiser*, 5 November 1914, p. 2.
[5] Information from Adella (Woogman) Moscovitz (daughter of Max) and Mrs. Joseph (Rebecca) Woogman, Vancouver, September 1977.
[6] "Trail Citizen Moves Here," *Bulletin*, 19 April 1968, p. 17; Leopold and Pearl Levey, taped interview by A. Krieger, Vancouver, 11 April 1973. JHSBC; and Leopold Levey, taped interview by C. E. Leonoff, Vancouver, 26 June 1976. JHSBC.
[7] Mary Biner, "Mrs. Leo Levey Heads Trail Hadassah Chapter," *Trail Daily Times*, 20 April 1942, p. 5; and "Mrs. B. Shapiro Organizes Hadassah Chapter in Trail, B.C.," *Bulletin*, 1 May 1942, p. 3.
[8] Mrs. Samuel (Bessy) Wise, Clara and Charles Waldman, taped interview by C. E. Leonoff, Victoria, 14 July 1976. JHSBC.
[9] "Clara Wise Weds Charles Waldman at First Trail Jewish Ceremony, Sunday," *Trail Daily Times*, 26 March 1947, p. 7.
[10] Margaret Tooley (niece of Martha Walker), taped interview by C. E. Leonoff, Seattle, 23 July 1976. JHSBC.

## 8 NORTHERN INTERIOR

[1] A. J. Arnold, "First Auto Trip to the B.C. Interior and a Railway Land Boom That Busted," *Bulletin*, 12 September 1958, pp. 6, 42-44.
[2] Ibid.
[3] Mrs. M. B. Cohen interview.
[4] "Jacob Leith to be 93 Years on July 1," *Bulletin*, 17 May 1968, p. 8.
[5] Obituary, *Bulletin*, 1 August 1969, p. 4.
[6] Spaner and Dayan interview.
[7] Obituary, *Bulletin*, 21 August 1970, p. 4.
[8] Gorosh interview.
[9] Pellin, "Directors"; and "B.C. Pioneers Wed 50 Years," *Vancouver Sun*, 11 February 1955, p. 33.
[10] (Canadian Jewish) *Congress Bulletin*, May 1943.
[11] *Bulletin*, 28 April 1944, p. 4.
[12] Mrs. Charles (Lily) Graham, taped interview by C. E. Leonoff, Vancouver, 30 May 1976. JHSBC.
[13] "Prince George Minyan," *Bulletin*, 30 March 1961, p. 8.
[14] *Bulletin*, 4 November 1955, p. 1; See also A. J. Arnold, "The Jews of Prince George, B.C.," Ibid., 14 October 1955, p. 3.

## 9 YUKON: FROM KLONDIKE DAYS — ONWARD

[1] Rudolph Glanz, "From Fur Rush to Gold Rushes," *Western States Jewish Historical Quarterly*, vol. 7, no. 2 (January 1975): 103, from *Alaska-Yukon Gazeteer and Business Directory 1903* (Seattle: P. L. Polk), pp. 223, passim.
[2] Charles S. Rosener, a young Jewish merchant of Dawson, to Mr. and Mrs. S. Rosener (parents), San Francisco, published in San Francisco *Emanu-El*, 4 November 1898. Typewritten copy JHSBC.
[3] Glanz, "Gold Rushes," from Jessie S. Bloom, "The Jews of Alaska," *American Jewish Archives*, November 1963, p. 98.
[4] Information from Arthur Zimmerman, Vancouver, August 1975.
[5] Walter Mackay Draycott, North Vancouver, to Right Honorable William Marr, 8 May 1975. Copy JHSBC.

6 Louis Brier, "Last Will and Testament," 9 May 1934. Copy JHSBC.
7 *Bulletin*, 3 January 1969, pp. 1, 12.
8 Harold Koffman, taped interview by C. E. Leonoff, Vancouver, 16 August 1975. JHSBC.
9 "Koffmans Leave North After Many Years," *Whitehorse Star*, February 1957.

## 10 PIONEERS IN MEDICINE

1 *First Two Years*, p. 12; and *British Colonist*, 18 February 1863 to 28 May 1863, passim.
2 Information from Dr. Irving Snider and Dr. Maurice Fox, Vancouver, 1977.
3 Information from Mrs. Theresa (Blumberg) Kaufmann (niece), Vancouver, August 1977.
4 Obituary, *Bulletin*, 9 November 1956, pp. 1, 5; and Mrs. William (Rachel) Morris, taped interview by Naomi Katz, Vancouver, 8 June 1971. JHSBC.
5 *Bulletin*, 28 October 1938, p. 1.
6 Vancouver Jewish Community Chest, *Souvenir Book 1924-1929 & Annual Report 1928-1929* (Vancouver: The Printery, n.d.), p. 11.
7 From an address given by Dr. M. Fox on the occasion of the Jewish National Fund Negev Dinner honoring him on Israel's Twenty-Fifth Anniversary, Vancouver, 3 February 1974. (Typewritten). Copy JHSBC.
8 Dr. Maurice Fox, taped interview by C. E. Leonoff, Vancouver, 21 August 1977. JHSBC.
9 *Bulletin*, 21 June 1968, p. 6; and 13 December 1968, pp. 37, 39.
10 Leon and Liselott Komar, taped interview by C. E. Leonoff, Vancouver, 17 April 1976. JHSBC.
11 Dr. Irving Snider, taped interview by A. M. Freedman and C. E. Leonoff, West Vancouver, 10 August 1975. JHSBC.
12 Linda Johnson, Archivist, Government of the Yukon Territory, Whitehorse, to Dr. Irving E. Snider, Vancouver, 27 May 1975. Copy JHSBC.
13 Information from Dr. Irving Ziskrout, Vancouver, September 1977.
14 *Vancouver Sun*, 16 April 1953, p. 14; and *Province*, 16 April 1953, p. 5.
15 Gorosh interview.
16 Rome, "Jewish Pioneers"; and Klenman, "Pioneer Jews," p. 15.
17 Obituary, *Bulletin*, 29 September 1977, pp. 1, 4.
18 Michael Ratner, taped interview by C. E. Leonoff, Vancouver, 7 August 1977. JHSBC.

## 11 VANCOUVER: THE PREDOMINANT COMMUNITY, 1886-1977

1 See obituary, *Bulletin*, 3 May 1974, p. 6.
2 Louis Rosenberg, *Canada's Jews: A Social and Economic Study of the Jews in Canada* (Montreal: Canadian Jewish Congress, 1939).
3 See Julius Shore, "Vancouver's Jewish Community Emerged and Began to Grow," *Bulletin*, British Columbia Centennial '71 Ed., 9 July 1971, pp. 15-22, 24; and Shore, "Emergence of Vancouver Jewish Community in 1920's," Ibid., 17 September 1971, pp. 63-69, 71. This two-part series written for the JHSBC is referred to throughout this chapter.
4 I. Stein, "Samuel Lodge No. 668, Independent Order B'nai B'rith," *Vancouver Jewish Bulletin*, 15 July 1925, p. 4; *Jew in Canada*, p. 436; "Original Charter Vancouver Lodge 668," *Bulletin*, 21 October 1960, p. 3; and "Vancouver 668 Founded Here 64 Years Ago," Ibid., 12 July 1974, p. 17.
5 "Our Beneficiaries: Hebrew Aid and Immigrant Society," Chest *Souvenir Book*, pp. 18-26.
6 A. J. Arnold, "First Vancouver Zionist Society Given National Charter in 1913," *Centenary Ed.*, pp. 24, 44, 46.

[7] *Jew in Canada,* p. 234.
[8] Ray Morris, "Hadassah: 38 Years of Aid to Jews in Search of a Home," *Centenary Ed.,* pp. 22-23.
[9] *Jew in Canada,* p. 255; and National Council of Jewish Women, Vancouver, *Faith and Humanity,* 50th Anniversary Edition 1924-1974, 10 June 1974.
[10] Morris Soskin, "Vancouver Jewish Community Chest," *Vancouver Jewish Bulletin,* 15 July 1925, p. 5; and "Jewish Community Chest Organized in Vancouver in 1924," *Centenary Ed.,* pp. 58-60. Reprinted from Chest *Souvenir Book.*
[11] Shore, 9 July 1971, p. 22.
[12] "First Women's BB Group Founded in 1927," *Centenary Ed.,* pp. 34, 36, 38.
[13] "A Capsule History of the Jewish Community Council of Vancouver," *Bulletin,* 1 April 1955, pp. 18-22.
[14] "Vancouver Branch Canadian Jewish Congress Formed," *Bulletin,* 9 January 1942, p. 1; and Naomi Pellin, "B.C. Jewry Takes Its Place on the National Scene Through Canadian Jewish Congress," Ibid., 12 September 1958, pp. 4, 46, 62, 64, 66.
[15] *Weekly News,* 21 February 1930, p. 1. Reprinted in *Centenary Ed.* pp. 40, 55. For an earlier plea on this same theme see S. W. Golden, "Our Next Move: United Action," *Vancouver Jewish Bulletin,* 14 August 1925, pp. 1, 3.
[16] "Jewish Community Chest Affiliates with Vancouver Welfare Federation," *Bulletin,* 5 February 1931, p. 1; and "Jewish Chest Became Charter Beneficiary of Vancouver Community Chest in 1931," *Centenary Ed.,* p. 58.
[17] *Vancouver Presidents' List 1975-1976* (Vancouver: Jewish Community Fund and Council).
[18] *Bulletin,* 14 July 1972, p. 5.
[19] Ibid., 6 November 1970, p. 4; and 16 June 1972, p. 12.
[20] Ibid., 23 January 1959, p. 1; 18 September 1970, p. 11; 9 November 1973, p. 9; and 25 January 1974, p. 5.
[21] Ibid., 2 November 1973, p. 5; and 21 March 1975, p. 21.
[22] "Suburbs Hold New Year Services," Ibid., 27 September 1974, p. 15.

## 12 REPRESENTATIVE COMMUNITY LEADERS

[1] Published sources on David Oppenheimer referred to are: Kerr, pp. 266-67; Rome, "Oppenheimers"; *Jew in Canada,* p. 58; and Ann Rivkin, "David Oppenheimer, Mayor 1888-1892: A Time to Remember," *Westworld,* November-December 1975, pp. 35-36.
[2] James Skitt Matthews, City Archivist, comp., "His Worship David Oppenheimer Mayor of Vancouver 1888, 1889, 1890, 1891: From the Originals Preserved by Mrs. David Hirsch nee Miss Flora Oppenheimer," (daughter), Archives of Vancouver, 1934, p. 8. (Typewritten).
[3] See R. E. Gosnell, Victoria, *A History of British Columbia* (Lewis Publishing Co., 1906), pp. 370-71, for a biography of Sidney S. Oppenheimer, M.D.
[4] Sources on Samuel Schultz are: "The Jew in the Legal Life of Canada," *Jew in Canada,* p. 375; Biography, Ibid., p. 377; *Centenary Ed.,* p. 32; and Rome, "Herman Schultz."
[5] Obituary Louis Lieberman Rubinowitz (father), *Bulletin,* 28 March 1958, p. 2, also contains data on the son. Israel Rubinowitz was the first delegate from Vancouver to attend a Canadian Zionist convention, Montreal, on 1 February 1903, *Centenary Ed.,* p. 24. Louis L. Rubinowitz, pioneer general merchant in Vancouver and Steveston, B.C., died at age ninety-eight. See also Ibid., p. 11.
[6] See *Jew in Canada,* p. 237, for a biography of Gintzburger; Ibid., p. 254, for a biography of his wife Rosina; and *Henderson's City of Vancouver Directory,* vol. xv (Vancouver: Henderson Publishing Co., 1908).
[7] Ripstein (grandson) interview.
[8] Morris, "Hadassah," p. 22.
[9] Obituary, *Bulletin,* 10 April 1931, p. 1.

10 Pellin, "Women's Role," p. 19.
11 "Women's BB," p. 36.
12 Obituary, *Bulletin*, 12 May 1939, p. 1.
13 See *Jew in Canada*, p. 396, for a biography of E. R. Sugarman.
14 *Bulletin*, 1 December 1932, p. 1.
15 Pat Prowd, "This Super Salesman Knows How to Sell People to People," *Daily Province*, 7 July 1951, p. 26.
16 Obituary, *Bulletin*, 25 May 1973, p. 4.
17 Sam Rothstein in interview with Bob Markin, "Pioneer Zionist Recalls 60 Years in Vancouver," Ibid., Centennial '71 Ed., 9 July 1971, pp. 23, 25-28.
18 Obituary, Ibid., 24 September 1971, pp. 1, 4.
19 "B.I. to Dedicate Presidents Plaque," Ibid., 6 January 1961, p. 5.
20 Obituary, Ibid., 18 April 1969, p. 3.
21 John Reed, taped interview by A. M. Freedman and A. Krieger, Vancouver, 7 December 1974. JHSBC; and biography prepared by Bernard Reed (son), 1976. Copy JHSBC.
22 Obituary, *Bulletin*, 19 June 1975, p. 4.
23 For biographies of these men see: "Centennial Scroll Award to J. B. Jaffe," *Bulletin*, 13 June 1958, p. 1; Jaffe obituary, Ibid., 1 February 1974, pp. 1-2, 4; Hirschberg obituary, Ibid., 15 July 1955, p. 4; and Grossman, *Jew in Canada*, p. 391.
24 See "Labor Zionists Honored For 30 Years Service," *Bulletin*, 20 February 1959, p. 6.
25 "Joshua Checov Honored by Community Leaders," Ibid., 25 August 1961, p. 17; and "Joshua Checov Permanent President Israel Histadrut Campaign," Ibid., 3 March 1972, p. 5.
26 Obituary, Ibid., 7 February 1975, pp. 1, 4.
27 Edgelow's, *Who's Who in British Columbia*, 10th ed. (Victoria: Admark, 1969), p. 72.
28 "Jack Diamond's 25th Anniversary of Service to the Synagogue and the Jewish Community," *Bulletin*, 18 September 1970, p. 16; and "Provincial Leaders, Community Pay Tribute to Jack Diamond," Ibid., 30 October 1970, p. 11.
29 *Bulletin*, 28 October 1955, pp. 1, 8.
30 Ibid., 31 May 1974, p. 10.
31 Ibid., 24 April 1975, pp. 1, 6; and 3 June 1976, p. 1.
32 *Vancouver Sun*, 12 April 1977, pp. 1, 21-22.

## 13 VANCOUVER: THE ORGANIZED COMMUNITY

1 Jennie Morris, "Hebrew Aid and Immigrant Society," *Vancouver Jewish Bulletin*, 15 July 1925, p. 2; *Jew in Canada*, p. 236; and *Centre Bulletin*, 15 December 1928, p. 4.
2 Chest *Souvenir Book*, pp. 6, 18-21.
3 *Centenary Ed.*, inside back cover.
4 Arnold, "B'nai B'rith Family," pp. 30, 32, 34.
5 S. Petersky, M.D., "Zionism in Vancouver, B.C.," *Vancouver Jewish Bulletin*, 15 July 1925, p. 7; and Arnold, "Zionist Society."
6 "Vancouver Hebrew Free Loan Association," *Centenary Ed.*, p. 60. Reprinted from *Bulletin*, 8 January 1931, p. 1.
7 San Francisco *Jewish Times*, 23 May 1924, front cover, p. 4; and *Jew in Canada*, pp. 434, 436.
8 Bernard Postal, "One Hundred Years of B'nai B'rith History," *Bulletin*, 27 September 1943, pp. 8-10, 35-36; and "B'nai B'riths Role in America," Ibid., 28 September 1954, pp. 36-37, 40.
9 *Daily Province*, 6 May 1926, p. 15.

[10] Sources on the Achduth Association are: *Centre Bulletin*, 15 December 1928, p. 4; A. Miner, "Achduth Co-Op Society Gives Valuable Services to the Community," *Bulletin*, 29 March 1940, p. 4; A. Miner, Fin. Secy., "Vancouver Achduth Co-Operative Society: A Brief Resume of Eight Years Activities, as a Chartered Institution," Ibid., 20 February 1941, p. 2; Shore, 17 September 1971, p. 71; and Abraham Wosk, taped interview by A. M. Freedman and Clara Auerbach, Vancouver, 1974. JHSBC.
[11] Lillian Zimmerman, "National Council of Jewish Women: 34 Years of 'Faith and Humanity'," *Centenary Ed.*, p. 25.
[12] *Faith and Humanity*, p. 5.
[13] Arnold, "B'nai B'rith Family," p. 30.
[14] "New Centre Official Opening This Sunday," *Bulletin*, 16 November 1962, pp. 1-3, 6-13, 17-20; and "Record Gathering at Centre Dedication," Ibid., 23 November 1962, pp. 1, 6.
[15] *Vancouver Sun*, 12 November 1927, p. 7.
[16] "Decade of Service at Council Well Baby Clinic," *Bulletin*, 29 May 1936, p. 4.
[17] *Bulletin*, 28 February 1941, p. 2; and 13 May 1966, p. 4.
[18] Ibid., 1 February 1946, p. 1.
[19] Ibid., 26 July 1946, pp. 1, 4.
[20] "National Council of Jewish Women 5th Biennial Conference Report," Ibid., 3 June 1948, p. 6; and *Faith and Humanity*, p. 21.
[21] *Bulletin*, 28 June 1951, p. 6.
[22] Thelma Ginsberg, "Why a Golden Age Club?," Ibid., 9 April 1952, p. 29.
[23] "Vancouver Golden Agers at the Western Wall," Ibid., 7 May 1971, p. 16.
[24] Leonard Stein, *The Balfour Declaration* (New York: Simon and Schuster, 1961), frontispiece.
[25] Theodor Herzl: Father of political Zionism, and founder of the World Zionist Organization.
[26] Shore, 9 July 1971, p. 24, gives a vivid personal reminiscence of collecting the blue boxes in the 1920s.
[27] *Bulletin*, 8 June 1951, p. 1.
[28] Ibid., 9 September 1953, p. 7.
[29] Irving Fineman, *Woman of Valor: The Story of Henrietta Szold* (New York: Simon and Schuster, 1961), pp. 254-55, 267-70.
[30] "Queen Esther: The Original Hadassah," *Bulletin*, 26 February 1953, p. 2.
[31] "The Scope of Canadian Hadassah," Ibid., 10 October 1958, pp. 7, 8.
[32] Morris, "Hadassah," p. 22.
[33] "The Biggest Affair Ever Undertaken by Vancouver Hadassah," *Bulletin*, 25 September 1952, p. 5.
[34] *Bulletin*, 11 July 1958, p. 1.
[35] Lottie Levinson, "The Vancouver Jewish Administrative Council in Review," Ibid., 19 September 1940, pp. 12-13, 32.
[36] "Capsule History."
[37] *Bulletin*, 18 February 1955, p. 3.
[38] Sam Kaplan, "35 Years of Pioneering," Ibid., 2 December 1960, p. 2. See also, Ada Maimon, *Women Build a Land* (New York: Herzl Press, 1962), for a history of the pioneer working women's movement in Israel.
[39] Pellin, "Women's Role."

## 14 VANCOUVER'S PIONEER JEWISH BUSINESSES

[1] Information from Major J. S. Matthews, Vancouver City Archivist.
[2] Ibid.
[3] *Bulletin*, 21 October 1966, p. 4.
[4] Henry J. Boam, comp. and Ashley G. Brown, ed., *British Columbia: Its History, People, Commerce, Industries and Resources* (London: Sells, 1912), pp. 223-25.

[5] Ibid., pp. 98, 101-2.
[6] Obituary, *Province*, 20 September 1968, p. 34.
[7] Aileen Campbell, "After 86 Years Store is Closing," Ibid., 4 October 1973, p. 43.
[8] "Max and Harold Freeman to be Honored at Negev Dinner," *Bulletin*, 11 October 1957, p. 1.
[9] Alfred A. Evans, taped reminiscences of his father, n.d., Vancouver. JHSBC.
[10] "Harry Evans Pioneer of the Klondike Gold Rush," obituary, *Bulletin*, 15 June 1973, p. 4.
[11] Information from Mitchell Snider, Vancouver, 1977.
[12] Obituary, *Bulletin*, 15 June 1973, p. 4.
[13] Information from Sam Flader, Vancouver, September 1977.

## 15 EARLY RESIDENCES

[1] Shore, 17 September 1971, pp. 65-66.
[2] *Vancouver's Heritage* (Vancouver: City Planning Department for the Heritage Advisory Committee, September 1975), p. 41.

## 16 VANCOUVER: THE TRADITIONAL COMMUNITY

[1] "Reminiscences of Early Days," *Dedication of Schara Tzedeck Synagogue*, Vancouver, 25 January 1948, p. 81.
[2] Vancouver *Daily World*, 1 October 1892, p. 3.
[3] Philo, Vancouver, to Dr. G. Deutsch, Prof. HUC, Cincinnati, 17 June 1894. Copy JHSBC. Published in *Bulletin*, 40th Anniversary Issue, 27 November 1970, pp. 16, 18.
[4] Ibid.
[5] A. J. Arnold, "Some Hidden Pages from the Early History of Vancouver Synagogues," *Centenary Ed.*, pp. 10-12.
[6] Arthur H. Fleishman gives a concise history of the early years of Schara Tzedeck Congregation in *Vancouver Jewish Bulletin*, 15 July 1925, p. 8; "In Search of History: The Story of Our Shul," *Dedication Schara Tzedeck*, pp. 35-44; "Fifty Years of Schara Tzedeck," *50th Anniversary Year Book* (Vancouver: 5718, 1957): 26-30, 43-47; and Lou Zimmerman, "Congregation Schara Tzedeck is Vancouver's Oldest Synagogue," *Centenary Ed.*, pp. 13-16, 28. The next three paragraphs also refer to these sources.
[7] "Jewish New Year," from a Vancouver newspaper of 15 September 1914, *Centenary Ed.*, p. 28.
[8] For biographies of Pastinsky see: "The Story of a Man and His Community," *Dedication Schara Tzedeck*, pp. 22-25; Simma Milner, "Rev. Nathan Mayer Pastinsky: A Jew a Pioneer Has Lived Here," *Bulletin*, 20 February 1948, p. 4; and obituary, Ibid., pp. 1, 3-4.
[9] See *Jew in Canada*, p. 391, for a biography of Grossman.
[10] Shore, 9 July 1971, pp. 19-20.
[11] Mrs. Max (Dorothy) Grossman, "Ladies' Auxiliary Temple Emanu-El," *Vancouver Jewish Bulletin*, 15 July 1925, p. 6; *Jew in Canada*, p. 267; and Arnold, "Hidden Pages," p. 11.
[12] *Vancouver Jewish Bulletin*, 15 October 1925, p. 2.
[13] Joseph Simon, "Congregation Beth Israel: Centre of Conservative Judaism," *Centenary Ed.*, pp. 17-18.
[14] "Beth Israel Congregation's 16-Year Dream and Plan to Become Reality," *Bulletin*, 16 September 1948, p. 1.
[15] Obituary, Ibid., 29 October 1965, p. 11.
[16] Obituary, Ibid., 25 August 1961, p. 1.

[17] "Reform Congregation to Receive Historic Charter Tonight," Ibid., 23 July 1965, p. 1; and Rabbi Raphael H. Levine, "The Challenge of Reform Judaism: Cultivating a Spiritual Wasteland," Ibid., pp. 2, 8.
[18] "T. S. Dedication . . .," Ibid., 11 March 1976, pp. 1, 6.
[19] Dan Propp, "Searching for the Core of Judaism: A Look at Vancouver's Jewish Congregations," Ibid., 17 April 1970, pp. 49-53, *Sephardic* pp. 52-53.
[20] *Bulletin,* 8 September 1977, p. 11.
[21] Shore, 17 September 1971, p. 63.
[22] Gertrude Weinrobe and Violet (Weinrobe) Franklin, taped interview by C. E. Leonoff and C. Auerbach, Vancouver, 25 July 1972. JHSBC.
[23] Obituary, *Bulletin,* 21 August 1975, p. 4.
[24] Shore, 17 September 1971, p. 64.
[25] Obituary, *Bulletin,* 3 July 1952, p. 3.
[26] "Schara Tzedeck Cemetery," *Dedication Schara Tzedeck,* pp. 82-83.
[27] Isaiah 25:8.
[28] "Official Opening of Chapel," *Bulletin,* 28 April 1944, pp. 1, 4.
[29] "1892 Yom Kippur Service Was Well Reported . . ." Ibid., 16 September 1955, pp. 8, 66; and *Centenary Ed.*, inside back cover. See also, Mrs. D. C. Hirsch, New York, to J. S. Matthews, Vancouver, 15 August 1945. Excerpt in *Centenary Ed.*, p. 8.
[30] Shore, 9 July 1971, pp. 19-20.
[31] *Centenary Ed.*, p. 8; and Arnold, "Hidden Pages," p. 11.
[32] Ibid.
[33] Weinrobe and Franklin interview.
[34] *Centenary Ed.*, inside back cover.
[35] Shore, 9 July 1971, p. 17.
[36] "Fifty Years," p. 27.
[37] Harold Kalman, *Exploring Vancouver* (University of British Columbia Press, 1974), p. 54.
[38] For information on Wohlgelernter, see *Bulletin,* 14 August 1930, p. 1.
[39] Exodus 25:8.
[40] "Hundreds Gather at Shule Site for Turning of First Sod," *Bulletin,* 7 February 1947, p. 1.
[41] *Bulletin,* 23 January 1948, p. 1; and 30 January 1948, pp. 1, 4.
[42] Shore, 9 July 1971, p. 20.
[43] *Bulletin,* 1 December 1932, pp. 1-2.
[44] "Pioneer Communal Builder S. W. Chess passes," Ibid., 7 February 1969, p. 4.
[45] *Bulletin,* 8 September 1949, p. 7.
[46] *Vancouver Sun,* 13 March 1976, p. 23.
[47] *Bulletin,* 12 March 1971, p. 3.

## 17 NEWS, LIBRARIES, AND JEWISH PRESS

[1] Klenman, "Pioneer Jews," p. 5.
[2] Rome, "Jews in Cariboo."
[3] Dr. J. I. Gorosh, "The Vancouver Jewish Library," *Vancouver Jewish Bulletin,* 15 July 1925, p. 5.
[4] *Centre Bulletin,* 14 October 1928, p. 2.
[5] Gorosh interview.
[6] "Editorial," *Vancouver Jewish Bulletin,* 15 July 1925, p. 1.
[7] Ben Chud, "*Di Yiddishe Velt* English-Yiddish Literary Magazine Founded in Vancouver in 1928," *Centenary Ed.*, pp. 42, 55.
[8] *Centre Bulletin,* 14 October 1928, p. 1.
[9] Ibid., 17 November 1928, p. 1; See also, "Pride of the Pacific Slope: An Account of Jewish Life in Vancouver 30 Years Ago Recorded in the Pages of the *Centre Bulletin,*" *Bulletin,* 12 September 1958, pp. 50, 52.

10 "Genesis of a Newspaper," *Bulletin*, 40th Anniversary Edition, 27 November 1970, p. 2.

11 See *Jew in Canada*, p. 178, for a biography of Goldston.

12 "*Bulletin* Has Grown from House Organ to Full-Fledged Anglo-Jewish Weekly," *Bulletin*, 25th Anniversary, 1 April 1955, pp. 3, 61.

13 *Bulletin*, 27 November 1970, p. 17.

14 Ibid., 1 April 1955, pp. 3, 61.

15 Ibid., 10 February 1949, pp. 1-2; and 27 November 1970, p. 9.

16 Ibid., 8 July 1960, p. 1; and 27 November 1970, p. 10.

17 Ibid., 27 November 1970, pp. 17, 20.

18 Ibid., 9 September 1976, p. 7.

19 "The Opening of Stanley Park," *Vancouver Historical Journal*, No. 2 (Archives Society of Vancouver, January 1959): 17-26.

20 Matthews, "Mayor Oppenheimer," Part 2, "The Oppenheimer Memorial," pp. 124-207.

## 18 EDUCATION

1 *Centre Bulletin*, 14 October 1928, p. 2. Her wedding was the first held in the Jewish Community Centre.

2 Stanley D. McLarty, "The Story of Strathcona School," Vancouver, May 1961, pp. 25, 32-33. (Mimeographed).

3 *Vancouver's Heritage*, pp. 47-48.

4 Chuck Davis, gen. ed., *The Vancouver Book* (North Vancouver: J. J. Douglas, 1976), pp. 252, 254.

5 "Pioneer Zionist," pp. 23, 25.

6 Shore, 9 July 1971, p. 18.

7 Norman and Florence Brown, taped interview by A. Krieger, Vancouver, 6 July 1971.

8 *Jew in Canada*, p. 184.

9 Shore, 9 July 1971, pp. 19-20.

10 *Vancouver Jewish Bulletin*, 14 August 1925, p. 2, gives a contemporary account of "The Talmud Torah."

11 Zimmerman, "Schara Tzedeck," p. 13.

12 "Vancouver Talmud Torah," Chest *Souvenir Book*, p. 28.

13 Harry Wolfe, "Thirty Years of Talmud Torah History 1918-1948," *Bulletin*, 2 September 1948, pp. 6-7.

14 See "Abe Rothstein Begins Fourth Term as Talmud Torah President," Ibid., 12 January 1950, p. 1.

15 *Bulletin*, 9 September 1948, p. 1.

16 Ibid., 14 March 1969, p. 3.

17 Harold Freeman, "Tribute to Abe Rothstein," Ibid., 16 September 1955, pp. 20-22.

18 Wolfe, "Thirty Years," p. 6; and information from J. Youngson, Vancouver.

19 See *Jew in Canada*, p. 317, for a biography of Zlotnik.

20 *Bulletin*, 30 August 1934, p. 1; 5 August 1938, pp. 1, 4; and 12 August 1938, pp. 1-2.

21 See Chud, "*Yiddishe Velt*," p. 42, for information on the *Muter Farein* and beginnings of the Vancouver Peretz School.

22 *Bulletin*, 29 June 1945, p. 1; and 24 August 1945, pp. 1, 4.

23 Inscription on dedication plaque.

24 Label Basman, principal, "Peretz Schools Aim is to Continue Jewish Culture," *Bulletin*, 22 September 1960, p. 20.

25 Information from Dr. I. Snider, Vancouver, 1977.

26 *Jew in Canada*, p. 396.

27 See Jack Piters, "The Far Western Menorah Conference," *Vancouver Jewish Bulletin*, 15 July 1925, p. 6, for the work of Menorah.

[28] *Bulletin*, 12 May 1932, p. 1.
[29] Ibid., 5 January 1973, p. 4.
[30] *UBC Annual*, 1916; and *Jew in Canada*, p. 237.
[31] *Bulletin*, 12 June 1970, p. 11.
[32] *B.C. Professional Engineer*, February 1971, p. 6.
[33] Biography JHSBC.
[34] Gerald Anglin, "Silver Images: Some Casting Back on the 25th Anniversary of Canadian TV," *The Canadian, Province*, 3 September 1977, p. 17.
[35] "Local Man Has Brilliant Academic Career," *Bulletin*, 7 June 1940, p. 1.
[36] Information from Harold Lando, Vancouver, 1977.
[37] *Bulletin*, 2 February 1945, p. 3.
[38] Ibid., 5 October 1945, p. 3.
[39] Ibid., 17 October 1947, p. 1.
[40] David L. Youngson, "10 Years of Hillel at U.B.C.," Ibid., 12 April 1957, pp. 5, 56.
[41] *Bulletin*, 28 September 1962, pp. 26, 32; and 12 July 1974, p. 17.
[42] Ibid., 9 November 1950, pp. 4-5.
[43] Ibid., 16 June 1972, p. 1; and 8 September 1972, p. 5.
[44] Ibid., 10 September 1971, p. 1.
[45] Ibid., 17 January 1964, pp. 1-2.
[46] Ibid., 15 March 1968, p. 1.
[47] Ibid., 9 November 1973, pp. 1, 12.

## 19 YOUTH

[1] Obituary, *Bulletin*, 22 May 1975, p. 4.
[2] *Bulletin*, 31 October 1958, p. 1; and "Centre Dedication," Ibid., 23 November 1962, pp. 1, 5-6.
[3] "Pioneer Zionist," pp. 26-27; and Shore, 9 July 1971, pp. 22, 24.
[4] Vancouver "AZA 119," *25th Anniversary Issue*, October 1954. (Mimeographed).
[5] *Bulletin*, 11 February 1972, p. 11.
[6] Ibid., 7 September 1950, p. 6.
[7] Levey interview, 26 June 1976.
[8] National Council of Jewish Women, Vancouver, *Program of Sixth Western Interstate Conference*, 7-10 June 1931, p. 16.
[9] *Faith and Humanity*, p. 7.
[10] Information from Mrs. J. (Bessie) Diamond, and Mrs. H. (Charlotte) Boyaner, Vancouver, September 1977.
[11] *Bulletin*, 28 January 1966, pp. 2, 5-8.
[12] "New Camp Hatikvah Opens . . . ," Ibid., 27 April 1956, p. 1.
[13] "Dave Nemetz Looks Back on 60 Zionist Years," Ibid., 4 May 1973, pp. 43-48.
[14] "Massada Offers Fine Leadership Camp," Ibid., 21 August 1964, p. 1.
[15] *Bulletin*, 13 May 1960, p. 5.
[16] "Salute to Habonim Youth Movement," Ibid., 18 July 1958, p. 1; and "Habonim Youth in the Local Jewish Community," Ibid., 10 October 1958, pp. 7-8.
[17] Amnon Hadary, "Habonim Camp Program Emphasizes Constructive Recreation," Ibid., 18 July 1958, pp. 4-6; "Camp Miriam Celebrates Its *Bar-Mitzvah* Year," Ibid., 26 May 1961, pp. 3-9; and "Thirty Years of Habonim Camping," Ibid., 1 June 1962, p. 5.

## 20 POLITICS

[1] *First Two Years*, pp. 52-105, gives a comprehensive dissertation on the career of Selim Franklin; See also, "The First Jew in Public Office," *Centenary Ed.*, p. 5.
[2] A. J. Arnold, "Aliens at the Door: The Path to Citizenship in British Columbia," *Bulletin*, Centenary Series, 2 parts, 8 November 1957, pp. 3, 6, and 15 November 1957, pp. 6, 8.

[3] *Jew in Canada*, p. 57.
[4] "Lumley Franklin: Mayor of Victoria," *Centenary Ed.*, pp. 5, 56.
[5] See *Jew in Canada*, p. 371 for a biography of Nathan.
[6] "First Jew in House of Commons," *Centenary Ed.*, p. 56.
[7] "Jews in Public and Political Life in Canada," *Jew in Canada*, p. 369.
[8] Arnold, "Jews of Prince George." The name was derived from Groman or Granovsky.
[9] Graham interview.
[10] *Prince George Echo*, 3 July 1958.
[11] *Bulletin*, 19 December 1958, p. 1; "Graham Seeks Fourth Term," *Prince George Progress*, 10 December 1964, p. 17; and Prince George *Citizen*, 14-15 December 1964.
[12] Obituary, *Bulletin*, 21 April 1967, p. 10.
[13] Sam Barrett, taped interview by A. Krieger, Vancouver, 26 March 1973. JHSBC.
[14] *Bulletin*, 12 June 1970, p. 1.
[15] "B.C. Elects Canada's First Jewish Premier," Ibid., 8 September 1972, pp. 1, 5.
[16] *Province*, 12 December 1975, pp. 1, 6-7.
[17] Patrick Nagle, "The Lamps Go Out After 1154 Controversial Days: Dave Barrett's Talk of Love Charmed Some, Enraged Many," *Vancouver Sun*, 12 December 1975, p. 12.
[18] *Bulletin*, 8 September 1972, p. 5; and 4 May 1973, p. 20.
[19] Ibid., 18 December 1970, p. 3.
[20] Ibid., 25 November 1976, p. 1.
[21] Information on Evers provided by Mayor's office, City of New Westminster, 1976.
[22] Simma Holt, *Terror in the Name of God: The Story of the Sons of Freedom Doukhobors* (Toronto: McClelland & Stewart, 1964). Jacket contains a biography of Holt.
[23] *Vancouver Sun*, 9 July 1974, p. 10.

## 21 WAR EFFORTS

[1] Sources for this chapter are: Pellin, "Women's Role," part on "Jewish Women in the War," p. 21; Lottie Levinson, Geneva to Naomi (Pellin) Katz, Vancouver, 17 May 1971. Copy JHSBC. Ms. Levinson was Executive-Secretary, Vancouver Jewish Administrative Council, before appointment to UNRRA, *Bulletin*, 22 December 1944, p. 1; Financial data on Federated Jewish Women of Vancouver. JHSBC; Mrs. J. (Bessie) Diamond, taped interview by I. Dodek, Vancouver, 20 May 1974, JHSBC; and Reminiscences delivered to NCJW Annual Meeting, ca. 1967. (Typewritten). Copy JHSBC.
[2] "176 Refugees Arrive . . . from Shanghai," *Bulletin*, 20 October 1949, p. 1.
[3] "Vancouver Jewish Refugee Committee Formed," Ibid., 21 June 1940, p. 1.
[4] "Local Jewish Women Do Their Share in War Work," Ibid., 10 April 1941, p. 10.
[5] "Jewish Women's Red Cross Unit at Work," Ibid., 12 April 1940, p. 4; and "Jewish Red Cross Unit Completes Almost 100,000 Articles Since Organization," Ibid., 3 March 1944, p. 4.
[6] Inglis, "Motor Car Man"; and Grossman interview.
[7] See *Bulletin*, 20 May 1948, p. 2, for biography; and "Negev Dinner to Honor (Mom and Pop) Waterman," Ibid., 20 October 1961, p. 1.
[8] *Bulletin*, 25 May 1945, p. 1.
[9] Philip Waterman, taped interview by C. E. Leonoff, Vancouver, 8 August 1976. JHSBC.
[10] "Waterman Family Represented in the Forces," *Bulletin*, 19 January 1945, p. 4.
[11] *Bulletin*, 6 April 1945, p. 4.
[12] Ibid., 24 August 1933, p. 1.
[13] Ibid., 26 June 1942, p. 1.
[14] Information from Mollie (Mickelson) Klein, Vancouver.

[15] *Bulletin*, 27 October 1949, p. 1.
[16] "Zlotnik Brothers Serve Country," Ibid., 16 March 1945, p. 4.
[17] "Jewish Veterans Get Legion Charter," Ibid., 8 June 1945, p. 1.
[18] *Bulletin*, 4 February 1955, p. 4.
[19] Leon Cheifetz, "Jewish Legion Attracted Canadians 50 Years Ago," Ibid., 11 October 1968, pp. 4, 11.
[20] *Bulletin*, 30 December 1948, p. 1; 22 September 1949, p. 3; Sam Morris, "Israel Re-Born: A Tribute to Ralph Moster," Ibid., 7 September 1950, pp. 28-29; and Ibid., 4 May 1973, pp. 4, 27, 29.
[21] "Vancouver's Valiant Volunteers Made History," *Bulletin*, Israel 25th Anniversary Ed., 4 May 1973, pp. 1, 8-11, 13, 20, 26-42.
[22] *Bulletin*, 8 May 1952, p. 1.
[23] Ibid., 1 November 1951, p. 1.
[24] Leo Levey interview, 26 June 1976.

## 22 RECREATION

[1] Information from Ruth Flader (daughter of Etta Goldberg), Vancouver, September 1977.
[2] *Bulletin*, 7 February 1969, p. 10.
[3] M. Soskin, *Vancouver Jewish Bulletin*, 15 July 1925, p. 3; and *Jew in Canada*, p. 451.
[4] Programme, *Inauguration Banquet of the Montefiore-Concordia Club*, Hotel Vancouver, 4 May 1929. JHSBC.
[5] Shore, 9 July 1971, pp. 22, 24.
[6] *Bulletin*, 19 July 1946, p. 1.
[7] Obituary, Ibid., 8 January 1954, p. 2.
[8] *Bulletin*, 12 January 1950, p. 6.
[9] Ibid., 18 January 1951, p. 4.
[10] Ibid., 24 January 1952, p. 8.

## 23 SPORTS

[1] B. Kaplan, *Vancouver Jewish Bulletin*, 15 July 1925, p. 3.
[2] Shore, 9 July 1971, p. 22.
[3] *Sunday Province*, 31 January 1926, p. 33.
[4] Jack Cowan, "The B'nai B'rith Athletic Association," *Vancouver Jewish Bulletin*, 15 July 1925, p. 8.
[5] Information from Saul Lechtzier, Vancouver, July 1977.
[6] Mrs. Philip (Rachel) Brotman, taped interview by C. E. Leonoff, Los Angeles, 29 December 1975. JHSBC.
[7] Obituary, *Bulletin*, 7 February 1969, p. 4.
[8] A. H. Fleishman, "Schaara Tzedeck Congregation," *Vancouver Jewish Bulletin*, 15 July 1925, p. 8; and *Jew in Canada*, p. 155.
[9] *Bulletin*, 29 September 1932, p. 8; and 13 October 1932, p. 4.
[10] "First Annual Cedarcrest Open Tournament and First Club Tournament," Ibid., 9 September 1948, p. 2.
[11] David Sears, taped interview by A. M. Freedman and C. E. Leonoff, Vancouver, 15 July 1977. JHSBC.
[12] *Bulletin*, 12 June 1952, p. 6.
[13] Ibid., 18 June 1954, pp. 6-7; and 25 June 1954, pp. 4-5.
[14] Ibid., 18 July 1958, p. 1.
[15] Information from dedication plaque at clubhouse.
[16] Sears interview.
[17] Ibid.

[18] *Bulletin*, 22 July 1955, p. 2.
[19] Ibid., 27 March 1952, p. 7.
[20] Ibid., 25 October 1957, p. 5.
[21] Brian Pound, "Freyda Berman Goes on Rampage," *Province*, 25 May 1957, p. 15; and *Vancouver Sun*, 25 May 1957, p. 19.
[22] *Bulletin*, 20 September 1957, p. 1; and 25 October 1957, pp. 1, 3, 5.
[23] *Vancouver Sun*, 10 January 1958, p. 18; and *Province*, 10 January 1958, p. 15.
[24] Ibid., 12 September 1959, p. 12.
[25] *Bulletin*, 15 August 1958, p. 1; 14 August 1959, p. 4; 19 May 1961, p. 2; and *Province*, 12 August 1961, p. 9.
[26] *Vancouver Sun*, 11 April 1966, p. 24.
[27] *Bulletin*, 11 July 1969, pp. 1, 8.
[28] *Province*, 10 September 1971, p. 14.
[29] Information from William Moscovitz, Vancouver, September 1977.
[30] *Province*, 13 February 1956, p. 19; and 5 March 1956, p. 7.
[31] "Into the Hall of Fame," Ibid., 7 April 1976, p. 2B.
[32] "De Luxe Bowling Alley Coming Up: Saul Lechtzier to Install Latest Thing in Alley Game," *Bulletin*, 10 May 1940, p. 4; and "De Luxe Bowling Alleys Opening New Year's Eve: Entire Proceeds to Red Cross," Ibid., 20 December 1940, p. 3.
[33] Saul Lechtzier, taped interview by C. E. Leonoff, Vancouver, 25 July 1976, JHSBC.
[34] Saul Lechtzier, President B.C. Bowling Alley Operators' Association to Chant Education Committee, 12 February 1959. Copy JHSBC.

## 24 THE ARTS

[1] *British Colonist*, 20 May 1859.
[2] Ibid., 23 May 1859.
[3] *First Two Years*, p. 23.
[4] *Jew in Canada*, p. 377.
[5] Tom Paterson, *The Victorian*, 31 May 1972, p. 7; and 7 June 1972, p. 8.
[6] Sources on Belasco are: David Belasco, "My Life's Story," *Hearst's Magazine*, March 1914 to December 1915; William Winter, *The Life of David Belasco*, 2 vols. (New York: Moffat, Yard, 1918), 1:2-15; *First Two Years*, pp. 24-28; David Rome, "David Belasco: A Canadian Jew," *Toronto Daily Hebrew Journal*, 21 November 1940; and Craig Timberlake, *The Bishop of Broadway: The Life & Work of David Belasco* (New York: Library Publishers, 1954), pp. 1-20.
[7] See Fawcett, "Reminiscences," pp. 29-31, 56, re school days in Victoria.
[8] *Nanaimo Free Press*, 28 September 1891, p. 1.
[9] John Cass, "Memories of the Old Opera House," Nanaimo, May 1975. (Typewritten). Copy JHSBC.
[10] *Jew in Canada*, p. 119.
[11] "Fifty Years of Schara Tzedeck," pp. 26-27.
[12] *Bulletin*, 5 August 1938, p. 1; and 28 April 1944, pp. 1, 4.
[13] Obituary, Ibid., 10 January 1975, p. 11.
[14] *Bulletin*, 12 April 1974, p. 11.
[15] Harry Woolfe, taped interview by A. M. Freedman and C. E. Leonoff, Vancouver, 8 July 1975.
[16] Les Wedman, "At the Movies," *Vancouver Sun*, 25 April 1969, p. 10A.
[17] Sam Kaplan, "Courageous Jewish Photographer Leaves a Priceless Legacy," *Bulletin*, Centennial '71 Ed., 9 July 1971, pp. 13-14, 28.
[18] *Bulletin*, 20 March 1931, p. 1; 24 April 1931, p. 4; 3 December 1937, p. 1; 29 March 1940, p. 1; 30 November 1945, p. 1; 14 November 1947, p. 3; and information from Alfred Evans, Vancouver, July 1977.
[19] *Bulletin*, 25 May 1933, p. 1.
[20] Ibid., 15 September 1944, p. 22.
[21] Obituary, Ibid., 28 October 1955, p. 1.

[22] *Centre Bulletin*, 1 December 1928, p. 1.
[23] Pellin, "Directors"; and Gorosh interview.
[24] *Vancouver News-Herald*, 31 August 1954, p. 3.
[25] "Directors Celebrate Golden Wedding," *Bulletin*, 18 February 1955, p. 5; and "Directors Diamond Wedding Celebration," Ibid., 26 February 1965, p. 6.
[26] "Directors Named Outstanding Citizens," Ibid., 13 October 1961, p. 5.
[27] "Zukerman's Bassoon Blows Some Beautiful Music," Ibid., 22 September 1960, p. 8.
[28] *Bulletin*, 26 March 1971, p. 5.
[29] Ibid., 29 March 1968, p. 12; and 4 August 1972, p. 12.
[30] "Centre Establishes Performing Arts Department," Ibid., 21 August 1964, p. 6.
[31] "An Orchestra is Born," Ibid., 27 March 1964, pp. 25, 34.
[32] See Cherniavsky interview by Sam Kaplan, *Bulletin*, 18 May 1962, pp. 5, 10.
[33] *Bulletin*, 22 April 1966, p. 10-A.
[34] Ibid., 16 May 1969, p. 12.
[35] "First Public Debut of Vancouver's Jewish Choir," Ibid., 2 May 1947, p. 1.
[36] *Bulletin*, 14 May 1965, p. 11.
[37] Ibid., 8 December 1967, p. 3; 14 February 1969, p. 8; and 16 May 1969, p. 12.

## 25 THE SUMMING UP

[1] British Columbia: 12,175; Yukon: 35, "Population Ethnic Groups," *1971 Census of Canada*, vol. 1, pt. 3, October 1973, p. 2-1.
[2] See "Focus on Vancouver Jewish Schools," *Bulletin*, 8 April 1971, pp. 25-41, 43, 45, 47, for a contemporary account of B.C.'s Jewish schools.
[3] See Arnold, "Aliens."
[4] See John Norris, *Strangers Entertained: A History of the Ethnic Groups of British Columbia* (Vancouver: British Columbia Centennial '71 Committee, 1971), pp. 243-44; and I. Wolfe, "The Jews," Ibid., chap. 9, pp. 117-23.

# GLOSSARY

NOTE: The words and phrases in this glossary are generally from the Hebrew or Yiddish languages.

Achduth: Union.

Agudace Achim: Organization of brothers.

Aliyah: Literally, to go up (to Zion).

Arbeiter Ring: Workingmen's circle.

Aron Kodesh: Holy ark; cabinet containing scrolls of the Law.

Ashkenazic: Originally German-Jewish; later applied to all East-European Jewish.

Aviva: Spring.

Bar Mitzvah: Literally, son of the commandment; a ceremony by which a male Jew at the age of thirteen assumes full religious obligations.

Bas Mitzvah or Bat Torah: Literally, daughter of the commandment, or daughter of the Torah; a confirmation service for girls.

Bet Chaim: Literally, house of life; a cemetery.

Beth Hamidrosh(ash): House of learning.

Beth Israel: House of Israel.

Beth Jacob: House of Jacob.

Beth Tikvah: House of hope.

Bimah: Pulpit; an elevated platform in the synagogue where the *Torah* is read.

B'nai B'rith: Literally, sons of the covenant.

B'nai Jacob: Sons of Jacob.

B'nai Yehudah: Literally, sons of Judah; mistranslated as sons of Israel.

Camp Hatikvah: Camp of hope.

Camp Miriam: Miriam was the prophetess who, along with Aaron and Moses, led the children of Israel out of Egypt.

Chanukah: An eight-day festival of lights, in which candles are lit commemorating the cleansing and rededication of the temple in Jerusalem by Judas Maccabeus.

Chason: Cantor, who leads the singing of religious services in the synagogue.

Chaver: Friend.

Chevri Chovevi Torah: Friends, lovers of the *Torah*.

Chevra Kadisha: Literally, holy friends; Hebrew burial society.

Chofetz Chaim: Literally, wants life; Polish *yeshiva* leader.

Chupah: Wedding canopy under which a Jewish marriage is performed. Made of fine cloth, usually silk or satin, held up by four wooden poles at the corners, it symbolizes the home, which is considered to be life's temple.

Conservative Judaism: Trend in Judaism developed in Europe and the United States in the middle of the nineteenth century, which permits modifications of service in response to changing needs, but opposes extreme changes in traditional observances.

Di Yiddishe Velt: The Jewish world.

Deutscher Shul: German synagogue.

Emanu-El: Literally, God is with us.

Gabai: Synagogue attendant; beadle.

Galut: Literally, exile; refers to the Jewish people living outside of Israel.

Ghettos: Segregated Jews' quarters in cities.

Habonim: Part of the world-wide Labor Zionist youth movement.

Hadassah: Esther.

Hagaddahs: Books containing historical stories, prayers, and songs recited during the evening meals on the first two nights of Passover.

Hatikvah: Literally, the hope; the national anthem of the State of Israel.

Hebrew: The language of the ancient Israelites. One of the oldest languages on earth; the earliest books of the Bible were written in Hebrew over three thousand years ago. After the conquest and dispersion of the Jewish nation, Hebrew was preserved as the Jews' language of prayer and religious service. It has been revived and modernized as the official language of the State of Israel.

High Holy Day(s): The two days of the Jewish New Year and the Day of Atonement, eight days later, are regarded as the holiest days of the year.

Histadrut: The General Federation of Labor in Israel, the largest Jewish labor organization in the world.

Jew(s): Originally one of the tribe of Judah; any person(s) of the Hebrew people or anyone whose religion is Judaism.

Judaea: Of or pertaining to Judah or the Jews.

Judaism: The religious doctrines and rites of the Jews.

Kibbutzim: Collective farm settlements in Israel.

Kol Nidrei. Solemn opening recitation at evening service on the Day of Atonement.

Kosher: Ritually fit to consume; food prepared according to the dietary laws.

Lag B'Omer: An ancient folk festival that had kinship with the forest and with the spring season of the year; an old custom is that of children going to the forest bearing archers' bows.

Litvak (Russian Litva): Jew from Lithuania.

Magen David: Literally, shield of David; the hexagram or six-pointed star, one of the most ancient symbols of Judaism.

Massadah: Situated at the top of an isolated rock on the edge of the Dead Sea Valley, Masada was Herod's fortress and the last outpost of the zealots during the Jewish war against Rome, A.D. 70-73.

Matzos: Unleavened bread; symbolic of the haste with which the Israelites left Egypt without waiting for the bread to rise.

Menorah: Seven-branched candelabrum, which according to the Bible was a prominent feature of the wilderness tabernacle, as well as the Jerusalem temple.

Meshulach: Delegate.

Mikvah: Pool used for ritual purification.

Minyan: The quorum of ten adult male Jews required for religious service; no congregational prayers or rites can begin until there is a *minyan*.

Mizrachi: Literally, spiritual centre; East; an Orthodox Zionist movement.

Mohel: Man who performs circumcisions according to religious ritual.

Muter Farein: Mothers' club.

Negev Dinner: An annual testimonial dinner sponsored by the Jewish National Fund of Canada in honor of a benefactor to the community and to Israel.

Orthodox Judaism (Orthodoxy): Modern term for the strictly traditional sector of Judaism.

Passover: The eight-day spring holiday, which commemorates Israel's deliverance from enslavement in Egypt over 3200 years ago, as recounted in the book of Exodus.

Poalei Zion: Movement based upon the Jewish proletariat, whose ideology consisted of a combination of Zionism and socialism.

Pogroms: A Russian word describing the attacks, accompanied by bloodshed and looting, against the Jews.

Purim: Festival commemorating the delivery of the Jews of Persia from Haman's plot to kill them, based on events described in the book of Esther.

Reform (Liberal) Judaism: Modern interpretation of Judaism, which emerged in Germany in the early nineteenth century in response to the changed political and cultural conditions brought about by the emancipation.

Rishona: First.

Rosh Hashanah: Literally, head of the year. The Jewish New Year according to the lunar calendar, which occurs in the fall of the year; a two-day celebration in which Jews gather together for synagogue service, prayer, and feast. The rabbis held that it commemorates the birthday of creation.

Schara Tzedeck: Gates of righteousness.

Seder: Literally, order; the ritual meal and service held on the first two nights of Passover.

Sefer Torah: Book of the law; the Pentateuch.

Sephard(ic)(im): Spanish (Jews).

Shammes: Synagoge servant; sexton.

Shneider: Tailor.

Shofar: Ritual ram's horn, which is blown as part of the service for the Jewish New Year, and at the end of the Day of Atonement.

Shokhet: A man authorized to slaughter animals or fowl conforming to *kosher* requirements, in order that it will be ritually clean according to the dietary laws.

Sholem Aleichem: Literally, peace to you!; a greeting. The pen name of Sholem Rabinovitz, Yiddish author and humorist of the Ukraine. His stories of Jewish life in Eastern Europe formed the basis for the modern musical production "Fiddler on the Roof."

Shul: Synagogue; school.

Sidurim: Prayer books.

Talisim: Shawls worn by male Jews during prayers.

Talmud(ic): The great body of Jewish teaching accumulated through the ages comprising ethics, religion, folklore, and jurisprudence, ranking next to the sacred scriptures in significance.

Talmud Torah: An educational institution to study the Jewish Law.

Temple Sholom: Temple of peace.

Torah: The Jewish scrolls of the Law containing the five books of Moses, handwritten by a scribe on parchment.

Tzedaka: Righteousness; justice; charity.

Yeshiva: Orthodox rabbinical academy.

Yiddish: Jewish language; vernacular spoken by East-European Jews, using the Hebrew alphabet but comprised largely of German words, with a sprinkling of Hebrew and other tongues.

Yom Kippur: Literally, holy day; the holiest Jewish day of the year in which men stand in judgment before God; Day of Atonement.

Young Judaea: Zionist youth group.

Zionism: Zion is an historic synonym for Jerusalem. Zionism is a modern nationalist movement of the late nineteenth and twentieth centuries to colonize Jews in Palestine for the purposes of religious and spiritual renaissance, and for the re-establishment of a Jewish nation in the ancient homeland.

Zionist: One who advocates and/or philanthropically supports the return to Zion.

# INDEX

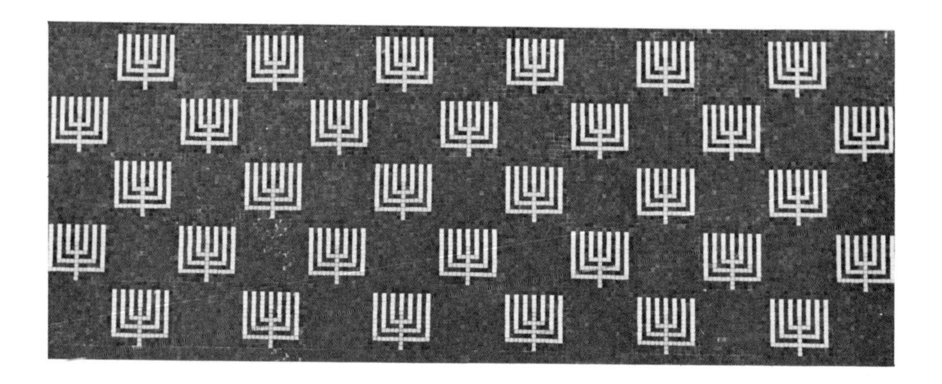